MW01622829

From *Referee* Magazine and
The National Association of Sports Officials

The It Factor in Officiating

By Jeffrey Stern, senior editor, *Referee* magazine

Cover design and layout by Matt Bowen, graphic designer, *Referee* magazine

Published by Referee Enterprises, Inc., and
The National Association of Sports Officials.

Printed in the United States of America.

ISBN-13: 978-1-58208-164-9

CONTENTS

INTRODUCTION

In all walks of life, there are people who have "It." It can take the form of knowledge, charisma, looks, ability or common sense. I have no data to confirm my belief that everyone has It in some way, shape or form. Nor do I know if It is God-given or is acquired. But some people have It and don't even know they have It.

The best officials in the world, regardless of sport or level, have It in spades. But every official has It to some degree. Officiating is part art, part science. It transcends both the art and the science.

This book is designed to help you understand It and help you increase your "It quotient." Several talented people — who have It when it comes to writing — contributed to these pages. They include Jim Arehart, Doug Day, Barry Mano, Jennifer Rardin, Dave Sabaini, Dr. Peter Sacco, Tom Schreck, Dave Simon, Tim Sloan and David T. Smith. The material in this book has previously been published in *Referee*.

Julie Sternberg, *Referee* managing editor, provided invaluable guidance and support.

I hope you find this book a valuable addition to your officiating library. That was certainly our goal.

Get It?

Jeffrey Stern
Referee senior editor

CHAPTER 1

THE ART OF BEING AN OFFICIAL

You know the rules and mechanics. Now it's time for the finishing touches. It takes an artist to become accepted as a good sports official.

Sports officiating is an art. According to Webster, "Art is the disposition of things by human skill." It is also "a special skill or power to perform certain actions acquired by experience, study or observation." On the other hand, officials make a "science" out of the study of rules and mechanics. In fact, they spend a good deal more time performing as scientists than as artists. Yet the most successful officials realize the importance of being an artist.

All officials must have a complete understanding of the rules and mechanics which govern their sport(s). The material presented here assumes that the official has that. Once, at a preseason clinic for men's college basketball officials, then-supervisor Johnny Overby began the first session with the following statement: "Every man in this room has a thorough working knowledge of rules and mechanics. Otherwise he wouldn't be here." From that the meeting's agenda moved on to discussion on the value of knowing how to cope with the human relations aspect of officiating. This chapter will do the same.

BUILDING A SCHEDULE

At first blush you might be asking yourself just what that topic has to do with the art of being an official. It has plenty to do with it. Having a good schedule means almost as much to officials as life itself. At first they struggle just to get enough games to fill their schedule. Of course, there is that competitive spirit which pushes them to work more games than the other officials they know. Once they have a few full-schedule years under their belt, they begin to get picky about which games they accept. Now another competitive urge takes hold: that of getting the "good" assignments.

The manner in which you proceed through those stages will be indicative of your own dignity. There are a number of things you should avoid when building a schedule. It may be quite difficult, but it will be better for you, in the long haul, to do them.

First, don't be pushy with the folks who mete out the assignments. Sometimes you can push for extra assignments, but the bad taste left in the assigners' mouths will not help you later. There are artful ways of letting them know you are available "on every day of the week ending in 'y,'" as the late NBA referee Roger McCann put it. Once you fill out the availability sheet or send in your closed dates, drop the matter. That will be one of the hardest things for you to do as long as you are an official. It always seems that the assigners don't give a damn about how long the official has to wait, on pins and needles, for next season's games.

Once in a while you walk onto the field or court and a coach comes up jabbering about some dates set aside just for you, for next year. The "class" way to handle that is to simply tell a coach to jot them down and send them to you the next day. Or suggest a phone call during the week. Under no circumstances should you engage in a discussion about future assignments prior to a game. Again, that is a toughie since your immediate reaction is to get those games ASAP. Keep in mind that if the coach really wants you on those games, he or she will follow up with a call or email.

WORKING TOGETHER

In his book *Modern Sports Officiating*, Bill Thompson states, "Building sound relationships with fellow officials, players, coaches and spectators while under the fire of intense athletic rivalry calls for an artist's touch." Often little thought is given to your relationship with your partner(s).

It is especially important to get to know each other prior to the contest if you haven't worked together before. When you first meet in the locker room, don't start blowing smoke about all the big games you've worked or about how you're being "scouted" by the pros. The best approach is to sit back, relax and let the other official enter the conversation. If you are very much the junior official, pay a bit of deference to your partners. Sure, they might look a little paunchy and their pants are short, but don't forget that some assignment-maker probably put them on the game to steady your nerves. In addition, they have most likely worked more tough games that season than you have in your entire career. If the assignment doesn't list your slot (position), offer the top one to the most veteran partner. For example, in basketball ask the veteran if he or she wants to be the referee. Naturally you would like the honor yourself, but you can help things jell by doing that. During the game, tell a fellow official when he or she makes a good call. Small things, yes, but powerful goodwill builders.

ON THE JOB

You became an official to officiate. That means you are charged with the responsibility of managing the game within the prescribed set of rules.

In the words of the late Richard Nixon, that is a "fundamentally true statement." But there is much left unsaid. Any contest officiated literally by the rules would be uninteresting to the spectators and more so for the players. The diversity of human athletic endeavors boggles the mind. There can be no set of written rules which completely governs a sporting contest. Human activity necessitates human judgments as to what is permissible. Enter the artist.

The official as an artist is the one who takes the gray areas of question and paints them decisively black or white, while making the interested parties buy the painting with little dialogue. Artists sell that painting with their very presence and obvious command of the situation. How can some officials do that while others would have to babble on about the technical merits of the work?

The artists recognize what the game and the participants are intended to do. You need to have considered just what the game is about. Former college basketball referee Irv Brown put it this way: "If the coach thinks you don't look like you've been in a jock strap, I guarantee you're in for a long night." You have to exhibit some savvy about the game. You aren't being hired to be officious, overbearing, authoritarian or a tough guy. You are being hired to enforce the rules, tempered with reason. That is a great word. You should be a reasonable person when officiating. When a testy situation arises, quickly ask yourself how you would handle it out on the street. Develop techniques to achieve your goal without having to invoke total dominance.

When you are watching games on the tube or as a spectator in the gym, don't worry so much about the judgment calls being made. Pay attention to how the officials are dealing with the many minor irritants that crop up in every game. Especially when you are watching televised games, note how the top-notch officials smoothly get their jobs done. There is a great deal at stake in those games, be they college or pro, yet the officials keep things under control more often than not. They seem to be able to talk players and coaches into being more reasonable. They don't get ruffled, red in the face, nervous or lose their tempers. They give the impression that "they've been here before."

Players and coaches respond very well to that type of treatment, but it is not easy to do. Under pressure scientific officials fall back on invoking the rules. They make it immediately known they know the rule and that's that. The artists, all the while knowing the rule, concern themselves with psychological aspects of the occurrence. They think, "How can I get the coaches back into the box (under control) and still hold their respect?" The artist realizes that since they carry the final authority in the matter, they may as well try to work it out and reserve the hammer for when it is absolutely necessary.

SELF PORTRAIT

There are very few people who think sports officiating is easy or an enviable avocation. The most commonly asked question offered to officials is: "Why do you do it?" Do you know why you do it? Multiple surveys indicate that money is not a primary reason. Mainly, officials do what they do because of their love of the game, the chance to stay in shape and the association with young people. Of course, you could have those things and still not officiate. We need to look further.

Personality studies have pointed out that as a group, officials exhibit a larger degree of dominance characteristics than the general populace. They like to be in charge. Once center stage, they enjoy having to make decisions under pressure. Additionally, they are very goal-conscious and strong-willed. All that must seem obvious to you.

What is the significance of all that? Those traits don't give the person the propensity to be humble. How many officiating associates do you know who would be classified as humble? Being humble is the exact opposite of being arrogant. The arrogant official might be more visible, but the one with a dash of humility will be more respected.

In conclusion, you might want to keep the following humbling thoughts in mind. If you have a solid schedule, give at least some of the credit to the officials who came before you and the ones who were nice enough to work with you. Don't forget to credit the "breaks" side of the ledger as well. When mingling with fellow officials who haven't advanced as fast and far as you have, why not let them talk of their hopes and aspirations? In turn, downplay how "great" your schedule is or, in fact, don't even broach the subject. Don't think for a moment that there aren't plenty of other officials who could do as well as, if not better than, you. Many of sport's top officials readily admit that those officials exist. They count themselves darn lucky to be where they are. Jim Tunney, then a top NFL referee and since retired, responded to *Referee's* invitation to be interviewed this way:

"Of course I will donate the time and energies necessary into making this a good article for your magazine. I guess there are some so selected who demand interview fees, but I don't happen to be in that league."

Imagine, the man who refereed conference championship games, Super Bowls, etc., commenting that he isn't in "that league." We can all learn from the humility of officials like Jim Tunney. He, along with many others, represents the true artist in sports officiating.

This Is It

When building a schedule, if you conduct yourself in a first-class manner you will come away with a higher opinion of yourself. In turn, that will affect how you carry yourself on the field or court. Make no mistake about it: Players, coaches and fans feel the presence of officials who handle themselves that way and your job will become easier and more enjoyable.

This Isn't It

Have you ever put yourself in a position that an onlooker would view as begging for assignments? Nothing can be more demeaning to you and the officiating profession in general than being perceived in that light. All sports officials are worth so much more than that.

CHAPTER 2

LOOK THE PART

You hear all kinds of stories after games. Among the close calls, the no-calls, the holds and the facemasks, other stories occasionally crop up that have nothing to do with player performance and everything to do with officiating.

One night, for instance, a member of a football crew forgot his shoes. That official was horrified about the prospect of working the game in his loafers. Luckily another crew member brought an extra pair that were almost the right size, so his buddy didn't have to look bad. Imagine what the coaches, players and everybody else at the game would have thought seeing the sideline official running up and down the field flashing a blur of brown tassels. It wouldn't have mattered how quickly and easily he got into position or how crisp his mechanics were, all anyone would have thought would be, "Look at that dumb official wearing dress shoes to a game." One look and his credibility would have been out the window.

One of the truest statements you'll ever run across is, "You only get one chance to make a first impression." Like it or not, officiating is a visual activity. (Extremely visual, in the case of televised games.) And while it would be ideal to have your work judged solely on its merit, good officiating involves more than a firm grasp of the rules and an ability to communicate those rules through mechanics. The choices you make before you ever step on the court or field can not only dictate how well you're received, but how far you advance toward postseason bookings and higher level assignments.

"If you don't look like a pro, you certainly won't be perceived as a pro," says John Clougherty, Atlantic Coast Conference coordinator of men's basketball officials and a former NCAA Division I official. "You want to look as good as you can," he stresses. "That's something you can do and have control over." Your look, of course, goes beyond simply being properly attired; you need to make sure your entire countenance and demeanor scream out professionalism and authority. Everything from the clothes you wear to your posture, gestures and facial expressions must convince everyone involved in a game that you're ready to officiate and that you take your job seriously.

Coaches, players and fans all carry enough verbal weapons that they'll occasionally aim at you. "Make sure you don't give them ammunition other than your game performance," says Clougherty. Toward that end, there is much you can do to enhance your presence on the field or court.

STAY IN SHAPE

We can all sit around and bemoan the fact that we're living in "the Age of the Supermodel," but the truth is, staying near your ideal weight fosters trust. Without ever speaking, you're saying you're serious about the event, willing to hustle and able to put yourself in the right position to make the call.

Any official has to be able to keep up with the sport he or she officiates. Officials have to do some running and some exercises in order to keep up with the players and cover plays.

DRESS FOR SUCCESS

An unkempt or worn uniform tells people that you don't take your role in the game seriously, and if you don't take it seriously, they won't take your authority seriously. So, wash out the odor, banish the wrinkles, polish the belt and shoes and replace worn equipment before the wear becomes obvious.

What you wear to the game also lends credence to the calls you make during play. Imagine that every game you work is an important job interview. Proper grooming is key. Keep your hair washed and neatly combed. Men should always arrive clean-shaven or with their moustache properly trimmed.

Most officials at the high school level and above arrive at the game site in business attire. Others wear dress pants and matching shirts bearing either the logo of their association or the conference in which they work. Either way you go, you're creating the impression that your mind is in the game before the game even begins.

If only officials were like elephants. It's easy to destroy the impression of alertness when you forget essential equipment. Many officials lay out their equipment days ahead of time and pack it the same way before every contest to prevent lapses in memory. When he was an active official, Esse Baharmast, now a technical instructor for FIFA, used a checklist, which he likened to that of a pilot. He says people feel more comfortable flying with a pilot who has a million miles under his belt, but they're not going to stay on the plane unless he checks the flaps before takeoff!

Frankly, preparing for a game is a completely acceptable time to be anal. You're not going to hurt anybody by reassuring yourself with three or four checks of your bag that everything you need is accounted for. If you're flying to an assignment, you want to fit everything you need into a carry-on (imagine arriving for a game in Indiana only to discover your uniform is traveling to Hawaii) so there won't be much room for extras. If you're driving, pack two of everything. Not only does that give you a backup in case of rips or breakage, it also comes in handy when your partners experience their own lapses in memory.

WATCH YOUR BODY LANGUAGE

How you carry yourself says more about you than anything you can say verbally. You want to exude confidence while appearing approachable and professional.

Randy Christal, longtime NCAA baseball umpire and football official, communicates confidence by holding his shoulders back and his head up. He feels you can exude overconfidence, even cockiness, with such subtle maneuvers as putting your hands on your hips or crossing your arms in front of your body.

"I'll talk to myself," Christal says, "(I'll say), 'Get your hands off your hips; get them down by your sides.'" At the same time, you don't want to appear meek. "Never look down," he stresses. Look down and you've fallen off the other side of the line, creating an aura of uncertainty you may be unable to erase. Keeping your head up while maintaining eye contact and holding your hands behind your back shows that you are in control without appearing arrogant or confrontational.

Be aware of how you run during play as well. An official should move in "cruise control." It's the ultimate balance between sloth and speed, making you seem neither lazy nor overeager.

Officials want to appear capable, but also want coaches to see they're approachable. When taking the court or field, the official who smiles, talks to partners and gives each coach a word of encouragement, accompanied by a firm handshake, will be looked upon favorably.

Other quiet messages of self-confidence include signaling sharply, maintaining eye contact, listening carefully and keeping your hands at your sides. Smile when it's appropriate but never frown or smirk. Practice a neutral facial expression that doesn't betray your emotions.

WALK THE LINE

Calling fouls or penalties seems cut and dried. After all, the mechanics are right there in your rulebook. But even if you signal correctly, be aware you may be adding extra moves that aren't in the book. When there is a foul, there must be a professional manner and a firmness in how you present yourself. You don't want to go through facial contortions. You never want to show excitement.

You never want to improvise either. "I think any time you put a lot of gyrations into it, you do it for one thing," says Clougherty, "and that's to call attention to yourself." He notes that you can sell a call without looking like a buffoon.

The opposite holds true: Be careful not to appear disinterested when making your calls. People will assume you don't want to be there or that you're too tired or bored by the contest.

ADAPT TO THE SITUATION

Though your degree of professionalism won't change from level to level or sport to sport, your approach might. You'll encounter less pressure at the youth level. Your demeanor may become more relaxed — but not lackadaisical. As you move up, though, the intensity rises exponentially.

AFTER THE GAME

Don't think that just because the game is over, your job as a professional is over. On or off the field, people will continue to view you as an official, so when the buzzer sounds, that's not an invitation to start scratching your armpits, light up a cigarette, remove your shoes and slump down on a nearby bench to air your feet. Your job begins when you receive an assignment and ends with the completed paperwork.

You wouldn't arrive at a game site wearing jeans and a T-shirt, so there's no reason to think it's acceptable to leave that way. After your shower, put your business attire back on and leave as you came. Until you're completely removed from your assignment — like when you arrive back home — you need to maintain your aura of professionalism.

Like it or not, people do judge books by their covers and officials by their appearance. You communicate a great deal about yourself and your abilities through your gestures, facial expressions and how you dress and groom yourself. First impressions are visual and you can make them work for you. Take it a step further and learn what body language you're speaking so you can walk the line without fear of falling off it. Work on maintaining composure, offering courtesy and stretching professionalism beyond the game. Treat every game as though there's a television camera following your every move and the importance of appearance will be second nature to you.

This Is It

If you wear compression shorts or similar garments underneath your uniform pants, tuck your shirt into the undergarment. It will help prevent the shirt from coming untucked during the game. Another option is wearing extra-long shirts, which stay tucked in better, and flex-belts to help keep them in place.

This Isn't It

Appearing bored, aloof or confrontational before or during the game sends a horrible message to coaches, players and fans. Stand with a slouch and your head down, avoiding eye contact with anyone, and you will be viewed as being timid or nervous. What about the official who arrives and stands with arms crossed while glaring at anyone who looks his or her way? That official appears confrontational. Better to maintain a professional bearing whenever you are on the field or court.

CHAPTER 3

ANALYZE THIS: SELF ASSESSMENT IN THE DIGITAL AGE

Admit it. We've all done it: You're watching a game on TV and a bang-bang play develops right in front of the official. You're not sure what happened, but a moment later the replay clearly shows there might have been a miss. "How could he have made that call?" you wonder, echoing the sentiments of the talking heads in the announcer's booth.

It sort of feels like you're sleeping with the enemy for a moment, but then your loyalties turn back to your officiating brethren and you remember the play you had earlier in the season. You remember it clearly — big play in the close game and the call was all yours. Of course, at least one head coach thought you blew it.

If you're like a growing number of officials, you're going to go to the film and check it out. Somebody will get you a video of the event and you'll slap it in the DVD player and see for yourself. You'll scroll to the pivotal incident, rock it back and forth once or twice, then slump back on the couch and hope that not too many of your friends were there to see you screw up like that.

So, what was the problem? You know the rules and have the experience to apply them and you're aware of the mechanics and how to practice them. But clearly you didn't take the right action on what is now screaming at you from the silver screen. The interesting thing is that most people who were in attendance — the fans and the teams — didn't know exactly what went wrong, they just cared about the unfortunate result. You, on the other hand, now that you saw your less-than-stellar positioning, probably know exactly what you should have been doing and should be able to apply that to what you see yourself doing in living color to learn what you could have done differently.

Those same digital images that so often crucify officials on the national television stage can also be our greatest resource in improving our lot.

Many teams record every game, and officials themselves often take advantage of that by furnishing schools with blank media to record the game and send it to the officials. But once you get it, what do you do with it?

The importance of videotape review can be broken down into two basic areas.

• It enables individual officials to see themselves, to watch their own appearance, movement and especially positioning. In a nutshell, you get to see what everyone else sees when they watch you work.

• It enables an official to see and study plays visually as opposed to the old tried and true (and still highly beneficial) methods of reading caseplays or mentally visualizing game action.

Officiating supervisors of professional leagues and college conferences do much of their reviewing from videos, sometimes looking frame-by-frame at particular calls — along with instant replay from differing angles — grading officials on every call they make and on violations that they miss. So-called amateur officials can benefit by looking at their own games, and associations that evaluate officials can surely do the same — as one official once said about viewing himself on a video, "You don't really know what habits you have until you see yourself exposed nakedly on the screen."

Officials are finding out that there may be no more powerful learning experience currently available than to evaluate themselves on video.

CRITICAL ANALYSIS

What is abundantly clear today is that the best individual officials and crew chiefs are making video review the cornerstone of their design for improvement. After all, pictures are worth a thousand words and seldom lie. And the biggest proponents preach a methodology for going through film to get the most out of it. Simply watching one play after the other, focusing on yourself as the key player, isn't going to cut it. Bill LeMonnier is a Big Ten Conference football referee and says you shouldn't watch film just to validate the calls you made; there's so much more to be gained.

"What we want to look at and break down on that tape aren't always just the penalty calls," LeMonnier explains. "We want to look at the plays to see certain mechanical things that happened, why they worked and why they didn't work.

"It's a talent like players have," LeMonnier adds. "If we can break down that analysis to whether it worked because we knew our rules, or because we had good mechanics, or because of the experiences we had in the game or our focus, we can use those criteria to say why a play worked or didn't work. We're going to be able to either continue to do it right or we're going to be able to possibly get it right and learn from our mistake.

"You've got to figure out why it broke down. If officials, as they look at that tape week-to-week can get into that discussion and share with their crewmates why did this break down? Why wasn't I focused? Why was I out of position? Then we're going to have a much better chance to get it right in the future."

A football crew, for example, works as a matrix organization. In any given situation, each of the four to seven officials working at the high school level or above is going to have a specific area of responsibility, which combines with others' to cover all the aspects of the developing play. If those roles are executed properly, there will be two — if not three — looks at the point of attack from different angles. Thus, if a play gets missed, LeMonnier believes it can be dissected by observing the covering officials and seeing what they weren't doing that they should have been. Maybe one official will be screened out but others on the play should be able to back them up and, if they still get it wrong, either the play defied the mechanics or one of the officials wasn't using them. The video will show the failure and the crew can decide what correction to make.

AHEAD OF EVERY SITUATION

There are many football supervisors or officiating scouts who can tell a lot about an official's mechanics by watching the bill of his or her cap. Officials in any sport seldom watch things on the field out of the corner of their eye. Thus, a referee covering a punter should have his cap pointed at the action around the kicker until everyone there has lost interest. Similarly, the back judge's cap should be pointed at the receiver and coverage, not at the incoming football. By contrast, if an official's cap isn't "on the play" you can tell a lot from where it *is* pointed.

Similar analytical strategies can be applied in other sports. A baseball or softball umpire will get the tag play right more often by

Tape Review Checklist

When reviewing an official's performance via video, consider these points so you can then look for them when reviewing.

- How does the official look? What does the official's run, walk and stance say?
- What is the overall read of the official's non-verbal communication?
- Where is the official on the floor (or field) in terms of coverage? Are they in the right place, or do they have the capability of getting to the right place?
- Where is the official's field of vision?
- How does the official look in relationship to the other officials? Is the official following a team concept in terms of coverage?
- How effective are the calls?
- How good (or bad) is the official at situational officiating, such as calls of consequence and the accuracy of those calls?
- The officials' overall game management skills.

You won't see all of those items on every videotape, but if you review a high percentage of games and mix up the various methods of video that you look at, you'll certainly find enough areas that will be helpful.

measuring where the tag is applied. To do that, the umpire has to have the right angle and a steady look, either of which will show up badly on video if he or she has weak mechanics.

In basketball, the crew is smaller than in football but the approach is the same, and an official can learn a lot by observing how each member of the crew was positioned on each play. Were they square to their area of responsibility and were they keeping their eyes on their own work? Were they flexing at the right time and were they maintaining their distance to get a good look? NBA official Violet Palmer believes that while mechanics will give you the best opportunity to see the play clearly, there is more than that to getting the calls right as you go up the ladder. You can use film to learn about the players and the game so the moves they make don't fool you.

"You definitely have to use your basketball instincts to anticipate where the players are going and to get in the best position," Palmer explains. "A luxury that we have in the NBA is that we have 29 teams. I will see every team at least three or four times, so for us we tend to learn our players.

"I know tendencies, I know personalities, I know my coaches, what my coaches do, what they don't like, which is an advantage for us because all of those small things help in getting plays right or handling situations correctly." Any official who looks at film can develop the same knowledge of the inner game, focusing on not only on themselves, but players and coaches, too.

Dave Yeast, an NCAA Division I baseball umpire and former national coordinator of baseball umpires, takes that study of the inner game even further. On a college or professional baseball field, very few things happen by accident and it follows that if you study the players on film, you can look for things they'll do to cause problems for you in a game. As an example, Yeast recalls a play from the 2006 College World Series in which a pitcher was caught on a balk at a critical point in the game.

The movement — a quick twitch of the knee toward home before a pickoff move to first — was caught by the first-base umpire. In analyzing the film, Yeast had edited the original TV feed to zoom in on the pitcher's legs and clearly show the problem. The obvious question was how the umpire was able to detect it and call it so definitively when it was hard enough to see on zoom and in slow motion. Yeast explained that the same pitcher was on TV about two weeks before and wasn't nabbed. Yeast was able to record the move, analyze it with his video software and show it to the umpires working the World Series as part of their briefing. So the first-base umpire was waiting for it.

Is that overstepping the purpose of video analysis? Yeast says no. Like LeMonnier and Palmer, he believes that modern video analysis has the ability to compress experience into a shorter period of time, letting officials do more to call the game correctly. And that's the key to successful officiating — keeping ahead of the situation.

But when it comes to analyzing your own performance — or anyone else's for that matter, if you are an evaluator or assessor — there are certain aspects of officiating that are key when viewing video footage:

1. Positioning and signals

Critically important to coverage of any play is positioning, so it should be first and foremost in your mind when analyzing your performance onscreen.Were you in the proper position to make a call? Were you screened out? Were you slow to cover a play, too close to the action? Signals are perhaps the most easily identifiable and easily assessed action on tape.

2. Subtle game rhythms

Beyond basic positioning and signals there are subtle things that establish, promote or interrupt a game's rhythms. Officials largely control that. Getting the ball back into play, administering violations smoothly and easing the game's natural intervals are all elements of game flow that you either enhance or deter.

3. Interaction with coaches and players

Take special note to how you react to challenges from coaches and players. Those behaviors are customarily "out in the open" for spectators to see, and the way you communicate with game participants is often revealed in your body language.

4. Minor game protocols

Do you look polished and professional during timeouts, when reporting fouls, when setting walls, retrieving balls or lining up free throws? Or are you self-conscious and awkward? Take note of how you appear during those routine game actions and see where you can improve your comportment.

RESPONDING SKILLS IN ACTION

There are other sports in which it's tougher for an official to use video to improve his or her performance. A good example is volleyball, where the referee remains pretty well motionless throughout the match except to signal the result of each rally. Success comes partially from making prompt, decisive calls on lightning-quick line or ballhandling situations. The referee and umpire on a match have to learn how to visualize and instantly identify the fine line between a fair play and a foul to build the trust of the participants and keep things from resembling the last moments at the Alamo. That touches on the other key factor in success, which is the official's finesse with responding skills.

"Responding skills" is a somewhat clinical term for managing the people in the game to get the job done without turning the contestants and their egos overwhelmingly against you. There's a premium on that in volleyball where the umpire is positioned between two coaches, each having the privilege to debate every call and the determination to do so. The umpire has to learn the proper response depending on the bait that is cast, and you can coach that with video if you also record what's being spoken.

Marcia Alterman, executive director of the Professional Association of Volleyball Officials, has taken the approach for several years of putting a wireless microphone on the umpire and filming the game from a low angle that continuously shows the two officials. It works because most of the bang-bang calls happen around the net anyway and the low view gives the officials a realistic angle when they review the accuracy of their calls. Also, every sweet nothing that is whispered in the umpire's ear and the response can be heard against the backdrop of the match.

Alterman cautions against officials "instigating" conversations. If a coach is going to tee off on a call, she feels they need very little invitation to do so from an official. Conversely, a coach is often busy coaching and wouldn't think to say something until cued by an unnecessary comment from the umpire. So the official is wise to concentrate on the proper response to what is said to him or her.

"You have to develop that fine art of knowing when I need to intervene and when, instead, I just need to move on," Alterman says. When she reviews videos with officials, she doesn't so much tell them what they should have said, but goes over the pattern of their responses to work toward more effective communication, as it's needed. And miking an official need not be limited to volleyball. The referee in football and basketball and the home plate umpire in the diamond sports are all people whose success depends on how they communicate with the participants.

TAKE IT TO THE NEXT LEVEL

It is more common nowadays for officials and their associations to develop platforms to use video as a training tool for the entire group — either "live" at association meetings or facilitated from a website. What's making that a practical reality now is the rapid evolution of editing software. For less than $100, user-friendly programs can be purchased that allow rather simple dissection of raw footage into useful training packages.

Years ago, you would have needed a film splicer and infinite time and patience to make a training tool on celluloid. Just 10 years ago, a reel-to-reel system for videotape would have been needed, but some unlucky soul would still have had to sift through it all to get something compact enough to use. Today, most editing programs can detect the natural breaks between plays where the camera was turned on and off. That allows the game video to automatically be broken down into a storyboard of vignettes that the editor can quickly sift through to get to the juicy stuff. The editor then has the luxury of categorizing and organizing footage almost as quickly as he can drag and drop on

How to Make the Perfect Video

Whatever the sport, there are right ways and wrong ways of obtaining a video that will be useful as a training tool by officials. Here are some of the things that the experts suggest:

Don't reinvent the wheel

In most cases, schools are only too happy to cut an extra copy of the game video that you're in — especially if it doesn't cost them anything. Many conferences use a standard format for video to facilitate film exchange during the season so your best bet is to find out what that is ahead of time. DVD is the prevalent one these days but there are still pockets of VHS. Take $20 to the store before the season starts and pick up a supply of blank DVDs and some bubble envelopes. When you check in with the athletic director a few days before your game, find out who the camera operator is and arrange to hand him the disc in a self-addressed, stamped envelope when you get to the game. Postage will be about $1. Then sit back and wait for the mailman.

Consider an upgrade

There are many schools, even at the high school level, that will provide things like interlaced end zone and sideline views of each play. In that format, you can see every official in at least one view of every play. In many other cases, sadly, what you tend to get is jiggly, too-close images that are partially eclipsed by the thumb of the student who shot the video. Back judges, the third-base umpire and the trail official all tend to disappear in the computer. The segments can either be spliced together into a continuous presentation or delivered episodically. The latter is a good approach for a website or email, where file size can be an issue.

Few things help develop an official better than to be able to watch esteemed colleagues go through their paces on video. Once the subjects of the clips get past the fact that they just might be spied booting a call, it can become a valuable learning experience

(continued on p. 37)

such efforts so you might want to consider having someone shoot a video just for you.

A spouse or friend, sufficiently bribed, can often be convinced to record the game on a broader perspective for you. Violet Palmer says she prefers an end zone shot that provides a sideline-to-sideline view of all three officials at the expense of a close look at the players. For football, consider a view taken from high in the stands above one goalline in order to capture all the crewmembers and better see "through" the play as the camera looks upfield. Wireless microphones adaptable to DVD cameras are very affordable, especially if you don't care about studio-quality sound. Spend a little time and effort in getting the most useful video in order to get more out of the product.

Get it from your association, conference or league

Does your local association have any kind of budget for video training? Maybe there's a subcommittee at your association made up strictly of members who have a strong interest in anything having to do with video or computers. Your group might be one that attempts to videotape games worked by its members for training purposes. Get your hands on any tape they have that shows you working. Or, as an alternative tap into your association's video library (if it exists). You won't see yourself on video, but there is still much opportunity for learning by proxy. The focus is on straight plays, as opposed to self-assessment, in that type of video training. The more an association can provide its members with that form of training, the better. It's accessible, it's fast and it's stimulating.

(continued on p. 36)

(continued from p. 35)

Record it from TV

That is certainly the easiest method, but unless you're a pro or a top college official, that method won't work for seeing yourself officiate.There is hope, though. With the increased number of cable channels available today, and the plethora of games being televised — especially high school games on local cable access channels — you may find one of your games on television (especially if you're lucky enough to be assigned a state tournament game). Take advantage of that when it happens. For the most part though, recorded games are for watching plays and for watching the mechanics and mannerisms of other officials. Keep your remote control in hand. Skip through the down time and the commercials, and focus on the plays over and over again.

Plan for how to present your product

Built-in software like Windows Media Player or QuickTime that comes with most computers these days is often adequate for reviewing video. Newer computers commonly have a DVD drive, too. That generic software will allow you to scroll through scenes and also give you some capability to cull significant episodes into separate files. For around $100, there is commercial editing software out there that will allow you to scallop and document the footage even more effectively and professionally for little investment of time. A computer-savvy crewmate or association member — or your 12-year-old — should be able to get that software producing results quickly. You'll be ready to go through the film yourself and, at the same time, save the funniest parts to a separate disc for use in a lighthearted training presentation. Also think about how you're going to display the finished product to an audience. You often need an adapter to display a computer video clip on a TV. Projectors that are compatible with computers are an alternative and many meeting halls can provide them. You can also simply burn a DVD of your assembled footage and play it scene-by-scene through a DVD player to a TV.

(continued from p. 35)

for everyone. Properly officiated plays work just as well as the botched ones and everyone benefits because learning to officiate is very much equal measures of seeing and doing. Video greatly accentuates the first half of that equation.

It is more than a little ironic that video, which was originally the bane of officials when used to document their failures, has now become perhaps our best tool. It stands to draw out the potential of officials faster by steepening their learning curve and that makes for more years of an enjoyable officiating experience. What will they think of next?

This Is It

When reviewing film with a group, limit it to no more than 20-25 plays. Beyond that, eyes tend to glaze over. Be sure some of the plays show good officiating. Don't dwell on the negative. Encourage your audience to look past the mistakes that were made (and who made them) and focus on the underlying principles and teaching points that will make them better officials.

This Isn't It

Don't let discussion during film review devolve into a long series of "what ifs." Too often that leads to once-in-a-lifetime scenarios that set eyes to rolling or divert attention from the matter at hand. Let the discussion go too far afield and you'll find the audience getting antsy or bored.

CHAPTER 4

THE 26 MOST IMPORTANT THINGS TO KNOW ABOUT OFFICIATING

What are the 26 most important things to know about officiating? The following statements, tips and advice presented in no particular order represent *Referee's* list and should serve as the foundation for any official's career.

1. DON'T MAKE EXCUSES

Even if you have the best possible excuse for making a mistake, the error won't be corrected because you have an alibi. Instead of wasting time and mental energy coming up with an excuse, your first course should be doing whatever the rules allow you to do to rectify the situation. Next you should learn from the mistakes so you won't make it — or have to come up with another excuse — again.

2. NINETY PERCENT OF OFFICIATING IS BEING A "PEOPLE PERSON."

Know how to handle people. Remember that listening is an important skill. If you're asked a question, answer it. Treat everyone on the field or court with the same respect you demand from them.

3. OFFICIATING IS SELDOM FAIR.

Regardless of how much talent you possess and how hard you work, you won't always work the big games or move up the officiating ladder. Officiating is one avocation in which sometimes it is less a matter of what you know than who you know. There is no use obsessing about things you can't control. No matter what level you work, you will often be criticized even though you are 100 percent correct. That isn't fair, but it's another facet of the job you must accept.

4. KEEP PLAYER SAFETY NUMBER ONE.

The rules not only empower but also require officials to penalize rough play. Even if a potentially dangerous situation is not specifically covered in the rules, an official is obligated to make whatever correction is necessary to ensure player safety. That entails everything from the weather to the playing surface to conduct of participants. In this overly litigious age, erring on the side of safety is not only the morally correct course but the one that will help keep the official out of court as well.

5. UNDERSTAND THE INTENT OF THE RULES NOT JUST THE RULE.

Knowing why a rule is needed will help you enforce it. In some cases, the intent is obvious (e.g. player safety). In other instances, a rule is intended to ensure that neither team or athlete is placed at an unfair disadvantage. For example, the infield fly rule in baseball and softball is designed to prevent the defense from achieving an undeserved double play. Ineligible receivers in football are prohibited from going downfield on pass plays so the defense isn't confused into thinking the player needs to be covered.

6. YOU HAVE AN OBLIGATION TO HOLD YOURSELF TO A HIGHER-THAN-NORMAL ETHICAL STANDARD.

How you comport yourself away from the game is as important as how you act during games. Poor decisions or bad behavior in everyday life can eradicate all of the good will and good impressions you earn when you're officiating. Remember that integrity is defined by how you act when you think nobody is watching.

7. EXPECT CRITICISM AND LEARN HOW TO HANDLE IT.

Most comments from spectators, players and coaches should go in one ear and out the other. Granted, that's easier said than done. But turning a deaf ear to such criticism is crucial to maintaining focus and keeping a positive attitude. Constructive criticism from supervisors, assigners and veteran officials should be sought. If you solicit comments after working with a respected veteran, be prepared for what you might get. It's possible you'll find out you're not as good as you think you are.

8. OFFICIATING BUILDS SKILLS FOR A LIFETIME.

The qualities that make a great official are also the qualities that make a person a good employee, spouse, parent and friend. Teamwork, loyalty, sacrifice, study, decision-making, fair mindedness, accountability and honesty are just a few of the positive skills and qualities that can be learned, developed and implemented through officiating.

9. NEVER LET YOUR SIGNALS CONVEY YOUR EMOTIONS.

Too many officials view fouls or rules infractions as personal affronts. Instead of acting dispassionately, they allow their body language or voice convey that displeasure. Your facial expression and voice should not suggest you're happy or unhappy to be enforcing a penalty.

10. ALWAYS HAVE A PREGAME MEETING.

Just as athletes must warm up before competing, officials must prepare themselves for the job ahead. Even if you work with the same partner or crew day after day, a pregame meeting provides valuable reminders about how certain situations will be handled. Involving every crew member or varying the routine helps prevent monotony.

11. IF YOU'RE GOING TO BLOW THE WHISTLE, BLOW IT HARD.

In almost every situation in virtually every sport, the rules dictate that an official's whistle causes play to cease. Since that is the case, you might as well blow it hard. The concept holds true for non-whistle sports — make sure everyone knows it when you call time. A strong blast of the whistle conveys the message that you're sure play should be stopped. A weak toot casts doubt about your confidence and judgment.

12. UNDERSTAND THAT YOU WILL MAKE MISTAKES.

Sometimes they are dreadful mistakes, but we must accept them as an environmental hazard in an avocation that calls for us to make a multitude of split-second decisions under very stressful conditions. To expect perfection is too heavy a burden for any person to carry and ultimately will take the joy out of officiating for even the best official.

13. DON'T CRITICIZE OTHER OFFICIALS.

Under no circumstances should an official point out a peer's inadequacies or offer a negative opinion about another official to a coach or player. Let your work and the work of others speak for itself. If an official you've worked with or observed asks for a critique, be honest but supportive. If your opinion is not sought, don't offer it.

14. BE PROFESSIONAL.

No matter the level, dress the part; act the part. In officiating, a book is judged by its cover. Soiled, aged, discolored, ill-fitting and wrinkled uniforms and accessories cast a negative impression before a pitch is thrown or the ball is put into play. Your appearance before and after the game is also important. No, you don't have to wear a tuxedo en route to a game, but it is a good idea to dress a bit better than most people might expect.

15. KNOW YOUR ROLE.

You are part of a bigger package — don't showboat. When you need to sell a call, it's OK to give an emphatic signal. But actions designed to draw attention away from the players and onto officials are unprofessional and unacceptable. Use the standard mechanics and signals for the level of play at which you're working.

16. BE PREPARED.

Plan for the unexpected. Don't anticipate the call, anticipate the play. That sounds like a contradiction, but it's not. If you can "feel" what's coming and adjust your position or your visual focus to the right area, you'll see the play better and you'll have a much better opportunity to make the correct call. Good umpires know when to expect a squeeze play. Top basketball referees recognize the times a team is going to apply full-court pressure or change its defense. Football officials know when to expect a deep pass or a quarterback sneak. In soccer, you know when a team will play kick-and-run and when teams will attack the defense methodically. All of those things help you anticipate the play, not the call.

17. CONTINUING STUDY IS A REQUIREMENT.

How many times have you had to correct a partner who applies an outdated rule? Good officials read the rulebook often. The more often you read it, the more ingrained the rules will be in your mind. That's especially important if you work multiple levels of the same sport (e.g. high school and college) or multiple sports in the same season (e.g. baseball and softball). Attending camps and clinics allows you to keep up with changes in philosophies and mechanics.

18. BODY LANGUAGE WILL DO YOU IN QUICKER THAN A LACK OF KNOWLEDGE.

Sometimes it's less a matter of what you say than how you say it. In officiating, body language often speaks louder than words. Even a correct call will cast doubt in the minds of participants if you don't appear decisive. During dead-ball periods, don't stand with your arms folded or shoulders slumped, which gives the impression you're bored or would rather be anywhere else.

19. POUR NO GASOLINE.

Coaches, players and fans will say plenty during most games. Much is designed to do no more than vent frustration. Understanding which comments or questions merit a response is a key to success in officiating. Yelling in kind can turn a small brush fire into a four-alarm conflagration. More often than not, the "right" response will not be verbal. You might nod your head slightly, smile momentarily, glance at whoever said something, hold eye contact for a moment or two, shake your head, or hold up a stop sign. Each alternative communication has a particular meaning; learn to use them wisely.

20. YOU DON'T CARE WHO WINS.

One of the many sports myths accepted as fact is that the officials are predisposed to favor the home team. But an official should never use calls to favor either team for any reason. Impartiality is the foundation on which the officiating house is built. Officials must be blind to factors that have nothing to do with the game, including who wins or loses.

21. YOU MUST HAVE A REVERENCE FOR THE RULES.

Before you can understand the spirit behind the rules you must have an appreciation for them. That doesn't necessarily mean knowing them verbatim. More important is understanding how vital it is to properly apply the rules. The avocation suffers when officials ignore or misapply the rules.

22. DON'T CARRY OVER FEELINGS TO THE NEXT GAME.

It is crucial to treat each game as a new experience. If you work a game involving a player or coach you've had to penalize or eject, your demeanor and actions must convey the feeling that you've forgotten about it — even if they haven't. Even the appearance of punishing a coach or player for something that happened in the past will taint your reputation and perhaps ruin your career.

23. REMEMBER WHERE YOU CAME FROM.

If you've achieved your goal, it's easy to forget what helped you reach that pinnacle. Few officials make it on their own. More than likely there was a mentor, an assigner or a local association that gave you the boost you needed. You can repay that kindness by helping another budding official. You may impress some people by bragging about your success, but more than likely you will come across as a pompous blowhard.

24. YOU REFEREE WHO YOU ARE.

Your officiating personality is driven by your everyday personality. That's not necessarily a bad thing. But remember that extremes are often detrimental in officiating. For example, if your job involves supervising people, remember that you can't treat fellow officials, players and coaches the same as you do your employees. If you're in sales, you may have to tone down your personality on the field or court.

25. FOR ALL BUT A FEW OF US, OFFICIATING IS AN AVOCATION, NOT OUR PROFESSION.

Recognizing that will help keep your life in better balance. It takes time, hard work and study to become a successful official. But an official must not put officiating ahead of what's really important: family and work. Devote more time and energy to your family and your job than you do to officiating.

26. CARRY OUT YOUR RESPONSIBILITIES IN A WAY THAT BRINGS CREDIBILITY TO THE OFFICIATING PRODUCT.

Remember that saying that the best officiated game is one in which no one knows who officiated? It's bunk. Competent, professional and impartial officials deserve acclaim, especially from other officials. Think how the public's perceptions of officials would improve if every official remembered that they represent the entire profession every time they work a game.

CHAPTER 5

HOW TO NOT ARGUE

It takes a minimum of two people to have an argument. If one person chooses not to participate, that leaves the second party blustering in the wind.

It's not an easy thing to not argue. In fact, it takes more mental toughness, emotional control and good old-fashioned restraint than it does to go on the offensive and fire when fired upon. But if you can train yourself to remain above the fray when a player or coach desperately wants to go nose to nose with you, you'll be a better, more confident and more respected official.

Before learning how to not argue, let's make it perfectly clear that nothing written or recommended from this point forward is intended as a substitute for dealing with a problem head-on and using any and all tools in your arsenal to manage that problem. When a participant clearly steps over the line when trying to goad you into an argument, that's another animal and you should deal with that appropriately.

Rather, this chapter is all about managing personal conflicts before they get to the point when harsher measures are called for.

CONFLICTS ARE NOT ARGUMENTS

During a game, how many conflicts do you get into? Probably a lot and many you may not even notice. A conflict occurs when you are at odds with the goals of another person. Since the main goal of most everyone else on the field or court during a game is to win, you face dozens of minor conflicts just by doing your job.

A conflict is not the same as an argument, but a conflict can easily lead to an argument if it's not resolved quickly and effectively. That's the key to not arguing: Resolving conflicts before they morph into full-blown arguments. Consider the following:

• Conflicts are normal and likely to occur in all areas of life, regardless of whether you are officiating a game or doing anything else.

• Conflicts are good because they notify people that something is wrong and needs to be modified.

• Arguments are power struggles in which individuals become highly emotional and can possess hidden agendas.

• Because of the emotional elements, arguments cause individuals to lose objectivity and become very biased.

• Since arguments become biased, emotional and subjective, individuals in essence play to "win." Therefore, a loser is most likely to come out of the mix. Since no one likes to lose, arguments are most likely to turn unproductive, even ugly, and they never create a satisfactory resolution for both parties.

CONTROL THE CONFLICT

The best way to stay in control of your emotions when someone comes at you is to remain as objective as possible. In fact, one of the best ways to remain objective is to exercise "perspective taking." In that exercise, you try to put yourself in the other person's shoes and see why they are upset or argumentative. Your goal is to apply your empathetic listening skills to the situation and better understand what the individual is feeling. They think you blew the call and now they are really upset with you.

Empathize with how the other person is feeling. Put yourself in his or her head and read what they are thinking. That accomplishes two things. First, it shows players and coaches you care and are open to listening. Second, it gives them the opportunity to release some frustration, and the more frustration they release (again, without crossing the line), the more objective they will be when it's your turn to speak.

To sidestep an oncoming argument, you should deal with the aggressor in a positive, assertive manner. Letting people know they are valued, respected and that their opinions matter sets up a situation for positive conflict resolution. Here are some suggestions for taking control of a conflict before it turns into an argument:

• **Let the other person talk — and don't interrupt.** Have the courtesy to listen before you say anything. You may have made up your mind and there's no way you're changing anything, but by fully listening to what the coach or player has to say, you can at least empathize with the other person's viewpoint.

• **Using your own words, repeat the problem back to the coach or player.** That lets them know you heard them and that you understood them. It also gives them a moment to calm down. In some cases it might help them see how ridiculous their points are. For example, saying, "Coach, what I hear you saying is that even though you and I both saw number seven clothesline his opponent, I should ignore it because we've already blown the whistle on you four times and we haven't called a foul on the other team yet. Is that right?"

• **Don't debate judgments.** You should always remain objective and not try to justify judgment calls once you have made up your mind.

• **Limit discussion only to the most recent call.** When the coach or player brings up a play from earlier in the game, it's time to shut down the conversation. Make it clear that you're only willing to consider the current conflict; the past is history.

• **Remain assertive and decisive.** Avoid being wishy-washy with agreements. You're free to change your mind about a call, but it should never appear that you were talked into that change. And if you do change your mind, do it in a strong, decisive manner. The worst thing you can do is look like you're going back and forth with your decisions.

• **If you can help it, don't engage in any discussion when you're very angry.** Officials are human and you may see or hear something that really sets you off for whatever reason. You make your call and now the coach wants to "discuss" it with you. If possible, walk away until you've regained your composure. You've probably seen a game or heard stories in which a player gets ejected, followed shortly by the head coach, then an assistant, maybe a couple of other bench personnel follow. It's easy to see how a person's tolerance level would get shorter and shorter with each successive verbal assault. Situations like that call for an alert partner to step in, giving you a moment to cool your jets and let the adrenaline drain.

• **When discussing problems, focus on solutions.** For officials, that doesn't mean changing your call, but you might acquiesce to a coach's request to consult a crewmate or you might say something like, "It was a good no-call, Coach, but I understand your frustration and I'll keep an eye out for the sort of contact you're talking about."

ARGUMENT? WHAT ARGUMENT?

How does all that make you a better and more respected official? It's no secret that in most walks of life, the people who get respect and even admiration are not the ones who are most-liked or who are easiest to get along with. True respect comes when people feel they are dealt with honestly and fairly. You won't get that by getting emotional; you will get that by being assertive.

On the other hand, being assertive is getting what you want while making sure you avoid hurting people or taking advantage of anyone along the way. Furthermore, it sets up a situation in which people are heard, their opinions respected and both parties work toward a win-win situation. In order to be assertive, you need to be open-minded and flexible. Listen to what people have to say. Listen to your own instincts and always try to be honest and do what's right. Being assertive doesn't mean winning friends or trying to appease people. It means responding to adversity in an honest, open way so arguments never have a chance to seed. That way, you maintain control during the entire discussion and steer the conflict toward resolution, all the while allowing irate coaches and players to have their say and feel their points are truly heard. Everybody

(continued on p. 55)

The Sinister Six

Beware aggressors who exhibit signs of any of these six classic arguers' styles:

1. The Exploder — The fuse is lit and it's a short one. There's a quick, highly-charged explosion of blaming anger and then it's all over. Afterward, calmness reigns and the coach or player hopes that all is forgiven. The problem is people who explode tend to do so often.

2. The Silent Enemy — That classic technique is used to punish through silence and obvious rejection refusing to relate except through forced one-word comments. That style wastes vast amounts of energy, rarely solves problems and tends to breed more resentment.

3. The Look-Backer — When coaches you've seen many times over the years collect what they perceive to be personal attacks you've inflicted on them over the years, they will use them as weapons whenever there is a conflict. That kind of angry interaction typically moves very quickly from a present issue to rehashing the past, and problems are neither constructively addressed nor resolved.

4. The Chipper — Repeated confrontations about minor irritations are the hallmarks of this mode of conflict. And those brush fires never seem to end.

5. The 'And Another Thing ...' Attacker — In that scenario, a conflict is never allowed to end because one person won't let go until he or she has the final word. That kind of conflict signals an inability of at least one person to talk out things in a reasonable way.

6. The Button-Pusher — That type plays a potentially dangerous game: He or she knows exactly what to say and how to say it so the other person involved loses control. There is little chance for healthy conflict resolution because one person habitually strikes directly at the other's vulnerabilities. The real intent is to hurt and to cut off communication, not to solve a problem.

(continued from p. 53)

wins. That's a far cry from allowing a game participant to draw you into the conflict on an emotional level that quickly becomes a full-blown argument.

This Is It

When a player or coach initiates an argument, consider first that you may have made a mistake. If you did, it's easier to empathize with an angry player or coach. If you didn't, it's harder, but you can still do it if you try. Think back to when you were a player and you wanted to succeed so badly you often had trouble accepting a call even when deep down you suspected it was right.

This Is It

In conflict resolution, the best outcome is two winners. Your tendency is to fight to win. That's what you have to rein in. At the same time, you're charged with managing the game and you're not about to give up control, or even the appearance of control, to a game participant. How do you do that? By employing extreme self-control.

This Isn't It

Don't confuse being assertive with aggression. To be aggressive is to get what you want without caring about others or what you have to do to succeed — winning at all costs even if you're wrong. That's a great way to quickly make enemies, lose the respect of the coaches and players and even lose the respect of your fellow officials and supervisors.

CHAPTER 6

PERFORM UNDER PRESSURE

How do you respond to pressure? You're going to experience it when you work that rivalry game or face that critical evaluation. It's a part of officiating, and it can be nerve-racking and even jarring. But face pressure with the right focus and mind-set, and you will thrive under it and reach maximum performance. The clock is ticking down to less than one minute remaining in regulation time. The game is tied, 43-43. One of the coaches calls a timeout, so you stop play. The fans are on their feet and cheering. The tension is mounting. It is one the biggest games you've ever had. The ramifications of victory versus defeat for the teams and your officiating career seem magnified. You need to collect yourself. You need to stay focused. You can't remember ever feeling this much pressure.

Why is the pressure getting to you? You try to quickly make sense of your scattered and fragmented feelings. Then you remember … things are going to get dicey in the next 58 seconds. Players will do anything and everything to win. They may think they can get away with more. But that's where you come in. Just as players will be expected to do their jobs to ensure success, so must you do your job and make the tough foul call when the game is on the line.

Are you ready to handle that kind of pressure? Can you feel your heart racing, blood pumping, sweat beading? Do you have the composure and enough oxygen to blow your whistle? Tick, tock, tick, tock, the timeout is over. Let the last minute — and the pressure — begin!

What do you think about when you hear the word pressure? Everyone in all walks of life in all careers face pressures in some form. What were you taught about pressure? Was it portrayed as "good" or "bad"? You will often hear people claim they do their best work and give their ultimate performances when faced with pressure. For some, pressure is the catalyst or straw that stirs their proverbial drink. Conversely, you will hear about many others who collapse, fold and crumble when faced with the same kinds of pressures.

What type of person are you? Moreover, what type of referee are you? Are you the pressure seeker / lover or adversity avoider? You need to be able to excel under pressure if you're going to thrive when making calls.

So let's get an understanding of the multi-headed phenomenon known as pressure. What is it? Perhaps the best way to define pressure in terms of competition or life is to perceive it simply as *stress*. Just like pressure, many a knee will buckle when people hear the ugly six-letter word *stress*! Both pressure and stress get a bad rap because they are often connoted in a negative light focusing on fear, failure and frustration. Too many people choose to focus and remember the worst instead of concentrating on the positive. Is there a positive to pressure, namely stress? The answer is *yes.*

There are two types of stress: distress and eustress. More often than not, it's the first type — the distress — that is more readily identified and avoided. Distress is caused by negative perceptions of events. Those events are usually fear-driven, anxiety provoking, intensely frustrating and have the ability to debilitate a participant. Translated … it's the whistle is in your mouth, primed to sound, you blow but nothing comes out — it's mute! In some ways the individual becomes frozen, both physically and mentally. The harder you try to respond, the less strength you possess. It's like your feet are immobilized in quicksand and your thoughts are in suspended animation. The funny part is, you literally stand outside of yourself and observe, trying to kick your own butt to try to move and respond. However, it often appears you are helpless to exert control over the situation. In fact, the harder you try to fix the situation, the more you screw it up. You start acting out of distress.

You become a responder or reactor rather than an actor or creator. It's like being in a gunfight with someone shooting at you whom you can't see. You respond by wildly shooting into the air hoping to hit someone. That is when the innocent get shot because your aim wasn't focused. In sports, that is when referees lose focus on the task and the game gets out of hand. They try to regain control by randomly firing and hitting something with their calls. Unfortunately, those officials lose control. They haven't gotten past what happened minutes ago when they made a mistake. That is acting out of distress and cracking under pressure.

On the other side of the coin is *eustress.* Have you ever heard of good stress or pressure? That sounds like a contradiction to many, but it exists. It is your interpretation of something that makes it distressful or eustressful. What might come off as disturbing for some might be pleasurable for others. Eustress is actually a very healthy type of stress. It provides a sense of fulfillment and is perceived as pleasant. Sound like competition and sports? You bet! Competition is pressure-filled. It's not about winning and losing for officials, but the competition of getting the calls right is there. And the achievement you feel after a good game is worth it. You are doing something you love and the endpoint (success) drives you. That makes the stressing (eustress) experience worth experiencing.

Where do you fit in on the stress/pressure continuum? Learn how to welcome the pressure and perform under it.

BACK TO THE BASICS

What is the best way to handle the pressures of officiating? It's the same as handling the pressures of sports as an athlete, the same as an accountant, lawyer, doctor, teacher, etc. — keep it simple, stupid! The intention is not to sound rude but rather obvious. The best way to handle pressure is to remain grounded. How do you remain grounded? When you use a simplistic approach, you are less prone to mistakes and seeing the game in panoramic view.

Most officials use their rulebook the same way some use their Bibles when they first start out … faithfully. Their officiating is on track. They can handle the pressures of situations as they arise. Problems arise when officials grow complacent and deviate from what they know and are taught. Want to control the pressures of officiating? You are armed with knowledge from the rulebook, teachers and fellow officials when you officiate. As a result, you are never alone. You have your conscious mind and unconscious mind. Conscious mind is your present mind-set and concerns over pressure. Unconscious mind is the collection of wisdom stored that is nonfeeling. Draw from the unconscious mind. With it, you are not alone when facing pressures.

KNOW WHEN TO FOLD THEM

Remember the famous Kenny Rogers' song from *The Gambler?* "You got to know when to hold 'em, know when to fold 'em." Of course Kenny was referring to cards in a poker game. Guess what? Emotions and pressure are like cards. After a period of time they will cause you to crumple if you don't have total control of the hand you're holding.

Sometimes the best way to handle pressure is to get away. If there is a moment during a game between you and a player or coach that is causing you to reach a boiling point, your best strategy may be to get the game started. Don't let them into your headspace. Give a warning or make the appropriate call and move on with the game. The game is bigger than you, and the player or coach in question. There are enough pressures associated with the game, and getting "personal" with athletes and coaches perpetuates the worst types of pressures an official can face — personal justification.

Don't run away from stress, because everyone has it. However, if you are in an overwhelming situation in which your performance or health is being jeopardized, perhaps the time is "now" to step away. Take a vacation and recharge your batteries.

LOOK AHEAD

They say hindsight is 20/20. And that is the truth. If we all knew now what we could have known then, we would all be ahead of the game — literally! Well, actually there is a way to see into the future. Visualization is an exercise that can be used to prepare for the game you are about to officiate. Just setting aside 10 minutes and mentally rehearsing for your event will do wonders. It is a relaxing exercise that allows to you to stay focused on how you want to act for the game. Successful professional referees and athletes have employed that method with great outcomes.

In your mind you prepare for situations that might arise, or ways you would like to see the game unfold. By mentally rehearsing it, you are training your subconscious on an experience that hasn't happened yet. You are teaching your subconscious how it should respond should that situation occur. It is basically like living self-fulfilling prophecies. If you tell yourself over and over you'll fail, you normally do, because that is what you set up the subconscious mind to do. If on the other hand, you visualize control, peace and success, that is what will unfold since your subconscious mind is tuned to that channel. Dr. Denis Waitley, a popular speaker and author of *Psychology of Winning* and other books, has used that approach successfully with Super Bowl champions, Olympic athletes and Fortune 500 executives.

Do You Know What is the Most Stressful Job?

According to *Health* magazine, the top five stressful jobs are:

1. Inner City Teachers
2. Police Officers
3. Miners
4. Air Traffic Controllers
5. Medical Interns

The same report listed foresting as the number-one least stressing career. You probably aren't interested in putting down your whistle to hang out with Smokey the Bear.

So how do people in stressful jobs handle their pressures? Are there skills those people use that officials can use?

Perhaps the best way to manage stress on the playing field, in the boardroom, grocery store, classroom or any job for that matter is to do the following:

1. Plan down time

Always make time for yourself to relax and unwind. You need to keep a healthy mind and body. Also, it is good to spend time with family and friends. We are social creatures who need support.

PUSH THROUGH THE TOUGH TIMES

Life will always deal you curve balls regardless of whether you are in the batter's box or behind the plate. The key to remember is it is just one moment in time. It will come to pass and there will be other moments. The best way to deal with tough times is to look at them as educational experiences. They prepare you to handle things differently and more productively the next time they occur.

It's not the tough times that stress and bend people. It's your attitude and how you respond. The famous "positive thinker" author Dr. Robert Schuller is best known for his book *Tough Times Don't Last, Tough People Do.* It's easy not to fail when you never

2. Meet with your supervisor
Try to meet with your supervisor at least every three to six months for feedback and input. Ask your supervisor to provide you with new insights, strategies or tips to help you perform better.

3. Manage your time
Most people complain they are always up against the clock and are always rushing. When you rush, you are more prone to make mistakes and are usually less or ill prepared. Show up early, have a coffee, read a book or meditate before your game starts so you are refreshed.

4. Keep things in perspective
Know that you have a job to do and to not take things personally. Separate the performance from "self." Criticism of your performance is not a stab at you as a person. It's when you take criticism too personally that you get stressed and become close to burnout.

5. Know when to say when
Never take on more than you can handle or more than you are comfortable with. That is putting too much added pressure on yourself and is setting you up for failure. Sometimes it is best to just walk away and take a break. Vacations are good.

attempt anything. There's not a lot of pressure involved either. But even in "failing," you never fail, according to Schuller. You learn and become better for it. Moments of pressure, stress and failure temper you and make you strong.

Knowing whatever you are going through will make you better for it is a great hope to hang onto. It helps to know there have been many other referees before you who went through similar pressures or worse and they rose from adversity and met the challenges.

IT'S JUST AN EXPERIENCE

Throughout your life, you will face pressures of every sort and intensity. Pressures and stress are good ... they let you know you're alive! If you have pressures in your sport, that's even better. It means you have a job and you are doing something you love or have chosen to do. Embrace pressure, push through it and enjoy it.

This Is It

Referees and umpires will face pressure in big games, such as state tournaments or rivalry match-ups. Pressure also comes with moving up a level or being evaluated. But officials should welcome those pressures and learn how to use them to get better and be successful. Remember the saying, "He who would be calm is one who gives the appearance of being calm." When all around you are confused, agitated or unsure, be the one who calmly takes control and sorts things out. It will boost your reputation.

This Isn't It

Don't obsess over how a mistake or possible mistake you made will affect your evaluation. You can avoid unnecessary stressful situations by concentrating on the events of the game. You have a job to do. So evaluations, fans, etc., should not even be a concern.

CHAPTER 7

CHART YOUR COURSE

What do you want out of officiating? The toughest games? To be the best? To move up a level? That's all within your reach. You just have to plan it out and follow through.

The purpose of a goal isn't necessarily to reach the goal. The purpose of having a goal is to motivate, to get you working. That's why it's important for any official — whether you're in your first year or 21st year — to always have a goal or several goals in mind for every season or every game.

Start by asking yourself some questions about what you want from officiating. It doesn't matter what level you are currently working, there must be a goal to every season that you are out there.

"I didn't know where I'd fit in when I first started," says NCAA Division I men's basketball referee Scott Thornley. "But I tried to survive as I progressed. The best officials are pleased with where they are and where they're going."

In many ways, goal-setting is all about survival and being in the moment. For Thornley, he found his way into basketball and officiated the 1996, '99 and '01 NCAA championship games. "Your (officiating) experience dictates where you can and cannot excel," adds Thornley. "You have different plateaus as far as ability and you can't get to the top of the ladder without climbing all the rungs."

Ted Barrett, an MLB umpire since 1999, said, "I was naïve in umpire school. I thought I'd do one year at each level (and then automatically move up). But once you understand the way it works, you can relax and then you're fine."

That is why it is imperative to keep a perspective on your own abilities and level of commitment.

So where is it that you actually begin? There are two general types of goals — outcome goals and performance goals. Outcome goals represent a standard of performance based on an event (like getting a particular game assignment, a playoff or big rivalry game). Performance goals focus on improvements in past performances (like running a better pregame conference or mastering your signaling).

Knowing your weaknesses and recognizing your failings will

help you determine which performance-based goals you should start with. Sincere failure is one of the most beneficial experiences. Know where your weakest spots are and focus on them. Without experiencing failure along the way in your career, you will never truly be tested to find out where you belong in officiating. If you take the path of least resistance, you might make it to whatever competition level you're shooting for, but you might never be a great official. We all learn from big mistakes. Do not be afraid to fail.

"To be successful, there is a certain comfort level that assigners, players and coaches need with you. People need to see you officiate in big games, tough games, to get that," says Thornley.

Goals need to be specific to be effective. A goal of "doing your best" usually does not achieve results. Instead a goal like, "I will remain absolutely calm when dealing with the coaches this game," or, "I will keep my eyes strictly in my coverage area this game," are specific and attainable.

Most performance-based goals are really short-term goals. Long-range goals are necessary to continue the chase of the ultimate goal. Look at your goals as steps. No one can leap from the first step to the top step. The short-range goals are the steps between where an official is now and where the official wants to be. Keep the long-range goal in mind because it is a motivator, but focus specifically on the short-range goals to get there.

Barrett, who was behind the plate for David Cone's perfect game in 1999, made his goals clearly defined as he moved up. "When I first got to umpire school in 1989, I set my goal to get to the next level. I talked to single-A guys before getting to that level, and double-A guys before then, and so on. When you're young, talk to the person who's closer to the next level. I may have the experience now at the major league level, but the system is different at each level and talking with the person who isn't so far removed from it can be great help.

"I (had) immediate goals and long-term or ultimate goals," adds Barrett. One goal was to umpire the second round of the playoffs, which he accomplished. "People always ask me about the World

Series," Barrett said. They stopped asking in 2007, when Barrett reached that goal.

Rules of Advancement

In 1991, Dave Witvoet, Plainwell, Mich., joined the ranks of the Big Ten football officials. It had been a long, hard struggle to get to the Division I college level since beginning in the high school ranks in 1972. He worked the BCS National Championship Game in 2006.

Network locally

"I never thought I would go as far as I did. But living in the area I do, I had many conferences and many people to help me along the way."

Look like you enjoy what you're doing

"I think you have to have fun and do well at the level you are working. Put yourself in a position to advance."

Remain approachable and open-minded

"Communication is the major criteria, with coaches, players and officials."

Be a sponge

"Rookies have got to work hard, listen and learn. Go to clinics and work as much as you can."

Keep it real

"Veterans, there is a level where you are not going to go any further. Be realistic and do the best job where you are. Go to clinics to help out the younger developing officials because you won't be in this game forever and you have to protect the future of officiating."

This Is It

If you've achieved one goal, set another one. That keeps you motivated and striving for constant improvement. If you've met your long-term goal of officiating in the college conference of your choice. Add another goal to get a postseason assignment. Each achieved goal adds on to the next one.

This Isn't It

Unrealistic expectations can keep a good official down when it comes to progressing through the ranks. They can foster a poor attitude or a sense of failure.

This Isn't It

In any goal-setting exercise, the essential part is knowing what it is you strive for, but it is counterproductive to aim for what is beyond reasonable. Want to officiate the Super Bowl? Sure. Who doesn't? Is it realistic? That depends. If you're an NFL official, you've got a pretty decent shot. If you're a high school referee nearing the end of your career, maybe not.

CHAPTER 8

GET YOURSELF ON THE RADAR SCREEN

They're watching you. Supervisors, assigners and observers are on the lookout for the best officials, the ones who'll go to state or to the conference tournament. They see hundreds of officials every season, but they only need a handful for the postseason. How can you stand out from the crowd?

Championship officials don't go unnoticed. Staying under the radar is no way to move up, whether it's in your work life, athletics or in the officiating ranks. The long-held belief in officiating circles that, "The best officials are the ones you never notice," is simply not true, and following it could leave you mired back in the pack.

There are thousands of games played on any given night. As regular seasons move through to postseason playoffs, the number of teams or individuals dwindles, as does the number of officials. In the end, there is a final contest and a champion is crowned. That's the one officials want — the big one, the one contest that determines it all.

There are a lot of ways to get noticed and not all of them are good. People will remember the official who wore all-white tennis shoes instead of the required black officiating shoes for basketball or the umpire who demonstrably calls every ball behind the plate. Individuals in the officiating avocation follow the traditional bell curve: There are a few poor officials, the ones who are sloppy in appearance, mechanics and rule application. There are a few outstanding officials, the men and women who stand head and shoulders above the rest. And then there is everyone else, the vast majority who call decent games, look fine on the field or court and who are just, well, serviceable.

How do you break out of that crowd and slide over into the rarified ranks of those on the right side of the bell curve? Sometimes it's the little things that make all the difference.

BE ENTHUSIASTIC AND HAVE FUN

Never forget that it's a privilege to have the opportunity to officiate a game. An official who meets with an athletic director who's grumbling about the autumn shower and declares, "If it's Friday night and there's a football game, it has to be a great night," will be remembered. Don't be afraid to smile or laugh, especially at yourself. Your status will be enhanced in the eyes of people who enjoy watching you work — who will see that you enjoy working. At the same time, don't act silly and don't forget when a more serious tone is called for.

BE EAGER TO LEARN

Keep a list of your strengths and weaknesses. In every contest, you should get better at one thing and find one other thing to improve the next game. Treat association meetings and clinics like a game. Attend, participate and walk away with new knowledge. If your local meetings aren't worth attending, do something to make them better. Watch others and adapt their strengths. Seek out and accept constructive criticism enthusiastically.

Officiate before and after the contest, and at all times in between If you start officiating when the game starts, you've already lost. You are onstage the moment you arrive in town. You are officiating in the parking lot, during pregame activities, during timeouts, while walking off after the contest and in the locker room. Anything you do during that time will reflect on your officiating. There is downtime in every sport. Just because the players aren't playing during a timeout doesn't mean you can lean against the bench. People can forgive and forget a bad call, but they'll remember if you look lazy and uncaring.

EXUDE CONFIDENCE

Make a good first and lasting impression. Cast a critical eye toward the way you look and act when reviewing a videotape of your game. Do you run like an athlete? Are your signals crisp and clear? Does your walk express confidence but not cockiness? Do you look angry when you make a call? Always take an athletic stance with hands off hips and never in your pockets. Never fold your arms across your chest. Don't try to seize command — earn it through your poise and presence. Establish and maintain a calm environment for the game. Nervous, edgy officials are easily spotted avidly chewing gum, pacing around or displaying a wide range of inappropriate emotions. Doing so prior to or during a contest will make you appear to be vulnerable to the pressure. Be decisive and confident in your decisions.

MANAGE YOUR BUSINESS

Treat supervisors, assigners, athletic directors and everyone else you have contact with as customers rather than bosses or adversaries. It's your job to make their job easier. If appropriate, call ahead of time so the school knows you'll be there — it's one less thing for the athletic director to worry about. If weather is an issue, call or email the athletic director to let him or her know the best way to contact you in case of postponement. Return contracts as soon as you get them, keep assigners aware of your available dates and notify the proper authorities if you have to change partners.

BE CREDIBLE ALWAYS

A football crew chief once handled a coach who was livid when an official blew an inadvertent whistle by marching over and saying, "Coach, we blew it, but there is nothing you can do to my linesman that will be worse than what we're going to do to him." Likely, he'll have no more to say. Credibility involves having a reputation for being believable, reliable and trustworthy. It has four basic components — empathy, honesty, expertise and dedication. Empathy may be your most valuable tool when it comes to stressful situations. The coach is under a lot more pressure than you might think. Understand and respect that. If you both know you blew a call, admit it. Besides, it's hard to argue with someone who agrees with you.

USE ADVANCED SKILLS AND MECHANICS

Over the years, our predecessors have come up with many ways to improve upon the basic mechanics. Take the initiative to learn those things by attending clinics and association meetings, reading about officiating and by talking to other officials.

BECOME A GREAT COMMUNICATOR

While an ambulance crew is loading a player onto a stretcher, officials are standing around talking and laughing. What's the message? Communication is an overused phrase, and not very well understood. It's not only about how you talk with coaches and players, it's every message you send though your words, your body language, the way you look at people and everything else. Officials should never stop communicating with each other and with the people on the fields and courts. Be firm when necessary, but use a normal, relaxed voice. Never bark. Shouting indicates a loss of control of both yourself and the game you're working.

NETWORK

A *USA Today* poll once showed that a majority of people distrust Congress but a similar majority trusted their own representative. People trust those they know. Get to know officials outside your immediate circle, assigners, coaches, athletic directors, some players (or ex-players) and even some spectators. Attend clinics and participate in your local and state meetings. Work scrimmages. File game reports and sportsmanship reports. Communicate with your state association, but not so much that you become a pest.

TAKE PRIDE

Do you strive to impress people with the quality of your work? Being great every game seems like an insurmountable task. It's easier to do something once. So be great once — over and over again. You will never achieve perfection, but the harder you try, the closer you'll get.

BE COMPETITIVE WITH YOURSELF

One of NASO's personal performance principles states, "The players give maximum effort; so should you — every game." Go into every assignment with the thought of giving the teams the best officiating they've ever seen. Try to never get beat, and always work hard to be in position. If you feel the game is below your status, don't work it.

Give it to another official, maybe a rookie, who will put in the effort the game deserves.

DO THE RIGHT THING

You're going to get booed anyway. You might as well get booed for doing the right thing. Make the unpopular call when it needs to be made. Eject those who need to be ejected. And don't back down to pressure from any quarter when you know you're right.

REAP THE REWARDS

You can stand out during the game by displaying professionalism, hustling, showing enthusiasm for your job, by having fun and working hard. Perhaps that is what that cliché about not being noticed really means — "The best officials are participants in the game rather than an interruption." Go beyond the norm and stand out. You might find yourself working the last game of the season when everyone else is sitting on the sideline watching the champions.

This Is It

Expect criticism. Most comments from spectators, players and coaches should go in one ear and out the other. Granted, that's easier said than done. But turning a deaf ear to such criticism is crucial to maintaining focus and keeping a positive attitude. Constructive criticism from supervisors, assigners and veteran officials should be sought. If you solicit comments after working with a respected veteran, be prepared for what you might get.

CHAPTER 9

THAT SINKING FEELING

Sometimes what seemed like a great call when you made it doesn't look nearly so good after you've replayed it in your mind two dozen times. And it sure doesn't help when every other person at the game seems to have seen something you didn't.

"If you stop for even a split second to think, that will interfere with your confidence."

Jack Childress, former Atlantic Coast Conference football referee and now the coordinator of officials in the South Atlantic Conference, makes that claim, and even routinely recommended to his crewmates that they turn their brains off occasionally.

Hold on. Isn't a mind a terrible thing to waste?

Thinking *can* be a bad thing for officials. Just ask any official who ever nailed a bang-bang scoring play late in a game. Crowd reaction — even if it's only coming from one side of the field or court — can be a powerful stimulus. The emotional highs brought on by the adrenaline rush from making your great call quickly fade when it seems every other individual at the game saw something completely different than you did.

That's when your brain kicks in and the sinking feeling starts: "Why is everyone screaming? I was in the right position and I had that call from start to finish. Sold the heck out it, too. No, I got it right. I'm sure of it.

"Well, I'm pretty sure of it. …

"Wait a minute! Did I blow that call?"

It only takes a few seconds to overthink and shake your own confidence. The worst part of a brain in overdrive? It pushes you into a mental downward spiral that is very difficult to pull out of if you aren't mentally prepared.

Childress experienced that feeling, he says, "a lot" over his long career. "You're ruling a fumble and recovery that goes against the home team, for example, because I know I've had lots of those," says Childress, "and everyone's moaning and screaming and you start to think, 'Gosh, there are thousands of people who didn't like that call and there's only one of me. Maybe I blew that.'

"Oh, yeah, I've been there lots of times," Childress continues.

"And there's only one way out — blow the whistle and get ready for the next play."

It takes no small amount of mental toughness to shrug off that sinking feeling, though. What's the best way to slam the brakes on a brain in overdrive and ease your concentration back onto the play at hand?

SNAP BACK IN SHORT TIME

Dr. Brad Beckwith is a sports psychologist in private practice from St. Louis who specializes in psychological kinesiology. He works mostly with baseball and football players, and much of his work has to do with emotional and mental skills training.

"I teach players to follow an acronym — ESPN," says Beckwith.

"E stands for evaluate (What is the situation? How much time is left? What are the possibilities? Where do I need to be? What is expected of me?).

"S stands for scan (Do I need to 'pump' myself up? Do I need to take a breath? Where do I need to focus?).

"P stands for plan (From that information about evaluating and scanning, what plan can I put in place?).

"And finally, N stands for neutral. Once the plan is in place, hit the enter key and let all of the physical, emotional and mental skills and abilities take over. Don't think; just respond to the task at hand."

There's that advice again — don't think. And really, during any sporting contest there is very little time to ponder anything before the action starts again.

"In baseball, I encourage players to go through that mental checklist after every pitch," says Beckwith. "If there's enough time for a young athlete to do that, adult officials can train themselves to do the same in the space between plays."

LIVE IT BEFORE IT HAPPENS

Completing the ESPN ritual and getting comfortable doing it takes patience and practice, but the key component, according to Beckwith, is in the "Plan" stage. That's when you need to refocus your brain to pull out of the spiral.

Mental practice and planning long before the game even starts is the key to success, says Dr. John Murray, a clinical sports psychologist from Boca Raton, Fla., who has worked with hundreds of athletes and wrote the book *Smart Tennis: How to Play and Win the Mental Game*. "Long in advance of a game, an official should anticipate any possible area of conflict, including self-doubt after making a tough call," he says. "Imagine moving quickly to the next play after taking a deep breath. The key to remember is that you still have a job to do. There is always another play coming up and it needs your complete attention. Otherwise your self-doubt could easily lead to a play that you clearly miss because your mind was elsewhere."

Childress relates that technique back to ground level. "I'm a big fan of (golfer) Jack Nicklaus," he says. "A long time ago, I was reading an article about Jack and he talked about how on every shot, he visualizes what it will feel like when the club face hits the ball. He does that before every swing; he would be totally consumed with that thought.

"We can do that, too. Visualize every play, not the easy ones that are black and white, but the gray area plays — roughing the kicker, pass interference, things like that. See them before they happen so you know which side of the gray area your call will fall on." Such visualization works two ways, according to Childress. The first is to help officials make better, more confident calls so they won't fall into a hole of self-doubt as easily. The second allows officials to snap back into the game when they do start slipping into that hole.

"I (used to) ask my crew all the time," says Childress. "'How do you work a perfect ballgame?'

"You work a perfect ballgame just like you eat an elephant — one bite at a time. Don't approach your work as if you're there to work a game; you're there to officiate that one play. And then the next one and the next one and so on. Eventually you will have officiated a whole game, but nothing is more important than the one job you have — the one play that's coming up. Never forget that every kickoff, every play, is only ever worked once. If you're still working play number 15 in a game, then who's working play number 16?"

MEMORY TRICKS

Why does that self-doubt creep in? You were fairly certain of what you saw when you made your call, but after numerous mental rewinds, the scene starts to change. What had been certain seconds ago is now ambiguous, maybe even dubious.

"Memory is very complex," says Murray. "If you ask seven people what happened at a car accident, you will usually get seven different accounts. And when uncertainty sets in, the mind has a way of filling in the gaps and getting creative. Second thoughts on officiating calls might become more common when the whole world is shouting that it was a bad call. Officials have a strong desire to get all their calls right — not just most of them, but all of them — and the external stimulus of a crowd in an uproar may make them question whether they were on the wrong side of a call. In general, though, there is usually much more accuracy in initial instincts than in afterthoughts."

Beckwith adds that the nature of officials to tend toward perfectionism makes them perhaps more susceptible to second guessing. "That desire to get it right every play makes officials put a lot of additional pressure on themselves," he says. "(But) judgment about any given call must be delayed until after the contest has been played. At that time, officials can look at the play and ask themselves, was I in a place both mentally and physically to make the call? Was I prepared to make the call? Sometimes everything is as it should be and an inaccurate call is still made. So be it. The key is when you are on the field, *stay in the moment*."

A technique Childress advises is to take the very thing that starts to make you doubt your call in the first place — the crowd noise — and use it to your advantage. "It doesn't matter if they're booing or cheering," Childress says. "Soak in the sounds of those hundreds or thousands of people and use it to pump yourself up. If you can't get excited by that many people who are all into the game that you're working, then I don't know what will get you going.

"That old line about loving it when they boo? That's true because all those people are right there in the game with you. And if you want to shut them up? Well, that's easy. Blow your whistle and move on to the next play."

THROW A LIFELINE

As a partner or a crewmate, it's usually pretty clear to you when your fellow official's mental wheels are spinning. The look on his or her face can be a dead giveaway and you can tell they're still looking at that last play. A good partner will act to help snap that official out of it and help him or her get focused for the next play.

"Get your crewmate's attention," says Childress. "Make good eye contact, flash him a smile and pump a big thumbs up in the air to him. It's just a little thing, but it shows you support him and you're confident in his abilities.

"If you have a conversation with an official, never ask him if he's sure about his call. He made the call, didn't he? Just ask, 'What did you see?' If there's doubt, you can talk through it. But don't spend a lot of time. Just get him ready to go for the next play."

If that doubt is swirling, it's especially important to control your body language. Often a coach will want an explanation of what you saw on that play and you cannot look wishy-washy.

Childress says, "Project confidence even if you're not. That coach doesn't need to know what's going on in your head. Fake it if you have to but do not slump your shoulders and look all uncertain." And then what do you do? Well, that's easy, says Childress. "You just take the next bite out of that elephant."

CHAPTER 10

13 TAKEAWAYS FROM EVERY GAME

Some officials go to a game, work it and go home, oblivious to the learning opportunities they missed. Across all sports, there are essential takeaways that you should remember. Don't leave your game without them.

Work even one season as an official and you quickly learn that you quickly learn. There are many aspects to working games that you don't read in rulebooks or manuals. But sit next to a wily veteran sometime and the wisdom soon pours forth.

Here's a list of 13 things every official should take away from every game. The list was painstakingly put together over the years through trial and error — mostly error.

1. KNOW THE MOST EXCELLENT WAY

With apologies to *Bill and Ted's Excellent Adventure,* the "most excellent way" refers to the best route to the game site. There is no substitute for allowing ample travel time to your game site. Who doesn't like arriving with enough time to find your host, changing site, partner and have a comfortable pregame? But veterans will tell you: It doesn't always work that way.

As often as not, you'll be leaving for a game from work without any time to spare. One good thing to take away from every game is what an old officiating buddy of mine called a "hair-on-fire" travel route. That is the quickest way to a given game site; a route where you may be less likely to encounter trains, traffic lights and speed traps. Officials who work frequently at the same set of schools often go home via different routes to see which is the quickest and offers the highest likelihood of a speedy trip when needed. A good route can be worth its weight in game checks. And speaking of checks …

2. MAKE SOME MONEY

We have all heard it said that officials don't "do it for the money." While that's true in many cases, the money is an important aspect of why we do what we do. And it helps to keep our families accepting of the hours away from home. The process of how officials are paid varies from area to area and even game to game.

If you are working a game and you are to be paid on site, get the check and sign all necessary forms before the game. Similarly, if the check is to be mailed at a later date, make sure that the host has all necessary information to expedite the process upon completion of the game. Reading the form carefully when you fill it out will help get the check in your hand in a timely manner.

When signing any form, be sure that it is returned to and secured by game staff immediately. Those forms often contain all the personal information anyone would need to cause you identity problems. Don't simply sign the forms and leave them on a chair or a desk.

3. LEARN FROM YOUR MISTAKES

Any honest official will tell you he or she is still waiting to work a perfect game — a game without any officiating mistakes, whether mechanical, rules-based or judgment. Since we all make mistakes, what should our mind-set be about them? Learn from every mistake you make.

When you make a mistake, after the game, first analyze what happened. Did you give a wrong signal or fail to signal at all? Did you rush instead of hustle? Maybe your error was a wrong call. What happened? Were you out of position? Did you anticipate the call instead of the play? Most importantly, what do you need to correct to make sure it doesn't happen again?

Teams like to hire experienced officials because they know those officials have dealt with all sorts of game situations — many of them being their own mistakes. Mistakes can and should be valuable learning experiences you can take away. Make the most of a bad situation.

4. NOTE WHAT WORKS

Of course, despite what most fans and some coaches and players think, most officials do most things right. The beauty of our avocation is that we can keep working on things not until we get them right, but until we don't get them wrong. Do you have trouble calling block / charge? What have you been doing about it? Have you increased your study of rules and films? Have you picked the brain of more experienced officials until you get it right? Congratulations! You did it!

Maybe you've been working on seeing outside pitches better, so you try a slight change in your plate stance and it works! Nailed it! Too often we fail to take credit for working on our game. If you try something different and it works, make note of it, share it and keep doing it. Come away with a sense of accomplishment.

5. JUDGE YOUR GAME TALK

Every game is not merely a series of calls and no-calls, it is also a series of interactions with players, coaches, partners and sometimes even fans. A sure sign of development in an official is how he or she handles the tough situations when a coach "comes out" on an official or a player decides to try to show him or her up. Inexperienced and insecure officials tend to "pull the trigger" early in those situations. Evaluate game conversations you had on your way home. How did you do?

It could be that you've had a tough time with a "problem coach," and you've spent time working on face-to-face discussions and conflict resolution techniques and this time things went well. Perhaps you were able to de-escalate a volatile situation and keep everyone in the game. Take an inventory: Why did things go better? What did you do differently? Replaying the one-on-one exchanges you had during the game will help you assemble a collection of techniques that will serve you well as you move up in your officiating career.

6. GET AN HONEST EVALUATION

We all know how important our pregame conversations with our partners are. But what about frank and honest postgame evaluations? Many officials at the collegiate level and above get instant feedback after every game on virtually every tough and many routine calls. That immediate evaluation serves an important purpose: It puts areas of your game that need work in the open and keeps them foremost on your mind. Sure, we all like to hear we did a great job, but the reality is every game gives us a chance for improvement.

Ask your partners how they thought you did, and then take their comments as constructive criticism. If partners are less experienced than you and reluctant to offer an evaluation, make it easy and safe for them to speak their mind by saying something like, "Remember that balk I called in the third inning? Would you have called that or was it picky?" Letting partners know that you have a question about one or two of your own calls will open the door for them to tell you if they saw something a little differently — and help you improve.

If your partners are veterans, they'll be more forthcoming, and sometimes a little more blunt, in evaluating you. Don't get defensive, make excuses or take it personally; take it as an opportunity for improvement. Keep that valuable means of evaluation open and take it home.

7. PUT IT IN WRITING

Sometimes we have to eject a player or coach and send a written report to the conference or state association office. About the only thing that can make that bad situation worse is to have to call back the offending school to get information you should have had before you ever even left the field or court.

Imagine having to call a still-agitated coach or athletic director and asking, "What is number 39's name again? You know, that kid I kicked out in the second half?" You'll be reliving the ugly incident in detail and with editorial comment before you know it.

If you have to file a game report (and you should for ejections, major injuries or unusual game occurrences), make sure you jot down all pertinent details as soon as the situation is under control and before you resume play. Taking that vital information home with you will surely save you and your assigner a major headache later.

8. GO TO THE FILM

Many high school football crews take a blank DVD and handing it, along with a self-addressed, postage-paid return envelope, to the home team coach before the game. They ask that the coach send a copy of his game tape, sometimes including an evaluation sheet they include in the packet. Crews that use that method may find they get a significant number.

What those crews discover is that coaches universally thought, correctly, that the officials take their duties seriously. They knew the officials were focused on doing a good job that game and improving from there. The evaluation sheets give the coaches a vehicle to vent (if necessary) before they ever have to submit a vote recommending the crew for the state tournament. It is a win-win situation.

When you get tapes back, you have a valuable and objective means of evaluating your own performance, free from the emotion and angles of the game. You get better that way.

Maybe you have a friend who could go with you to the game and record it in the stands for you. Perhaps your association has a system in place to get tape of you working games. Whatever it takes to take video home with you, it's worth it.

9. STAY HEALTHY

It may seem almost too obvious, but it's important: One of the biggest things you need to take home with you after a game is your health. As is the case with everything else in officiating, maintaining your health has many facets.

One official had a discussion with a college team's athletic trainer as teams were warming up before a game. The official commented on the time the teams spent stretching. The athletic trainer asked how much time the official spent stretching before walking on the field that day. When the official answered with a somewhat inflated, "About five minutes," the athletic trainer said, "If these athletes who are at the top of their game and at the peak of their physical condition and at least 10 or 15 years younger than you know it's important to stretch for 20 minutes or more, what makes you think you can get away with less?"

Officials spend countless hours reviewing rules, attending clinics and otherwise working on their game. But do officials invest more than the minimum in their health? Do they warm up and then stretch enough before games? Do they get enough rest? Do they eat properly in and out of season?

When you're working games, do you have the best equipment you can afford? Does it fit properly? All of those are small points, but added up, they make the difference in going home with your health — or not.

10. RETAIN TEAM TENDENCIES

They say, "Knowledge is power," and nowhere is that more true than in officiating. Whatever you can learn about teams and their tendencies, coaches and players during a game can provide valuable information that may prove useful as you call the next game you have with them. You can also pass the information on to your fellow officials who will see the teams next week, in the playoffs or at the state tournament.

While we certainly avoid "making up our mind" about a coach, or worse — a specific type of play or strategy — before a game, knowing how a team plays or what it tries to do simply helps prepare you to call the best game possible.

As you go home, use the knowledge you took away from a previous game and give some thought to your next game. As the saying goes, "Luck favors the well-prepared."

11. PICK UP YOUR STUFF

You're on the way home from a game. You're tired, hungry and want nothing more than to sit back and have a cold adult beverage. All of a sudden, your cell phone rings. "Uh, yeah, is this Mr. Official? Hi, I'm Billy, the team manager at the school you just worked. Mr. Athletic Director wanted me to call you and tell you he thinks you left your plate shoes here." Having another game tomorrow, you turn around, retracing the 10 miles you just drove and delay that much-needed beverage.

Remembering to take your gear with you isn't always as simple a matter as it should be. In many areas, especially during the spring sports season, officials change in parking lots, rest rooms and cars. Gear is placed on the roof of your car, the bed of your truck and on the ground. Get distracted or in a rush and your equipment can vanish like dust in the wind.

Develop a routine that is close to sacred when you gear up and down for a game, then don't vary that routine. Keep things in the same bag or tub every time so you know at a glance when something isn't where it should be. If you find yourself in a situation where you are changing "on the fly," for example a baseball rainout, put everything you remove in one place. You can inventory and clean it at home.

12. KEEP YOUR SANITY

No doubt you remember the commercial. The football official was getting a royal chewing on the sideline. The TV commentators were remarking what tremendous concentration the official had and wondered aloud where he developed such concentration. The scene then changed to the official's home where the poor fellow was enduring a similar dressing-down from his wife. Funny? Yes. But the reality is that officiating is a high-stress avocation. Don't let it cost you your sanity.

You can count on something going wrong just about every game. In some situations, you may have a coach who is ill-tempered and who is determined to send you home feeling like you just took a little girl's doll from her. Don't let that happen.

You need to go home with your sanity. You owe it to yourself and your family. If things go sideways at a game, settle the situation, then give yourself a short "self-talk" recognizing the fact that you got things under control and that the game is yours again. On your way home, relax, put the game behind you and walk in the door ready for your family. It's a crucial tool you must take home: the ability to decompress after a tough game.

13. TAKE PRIDE IN YOUR WORK

One of the most important things you shouldn't leave your games without is a sense of accomplishment, the knowledge that you not only performed a service, but that you did something very few people can do: You officiated a game, and you did it well.

CHAPTER 11

HOW WE MAKE THINGS WORSE

The old saying among officials is, the only friends we have out there are our partners and ourselves. If that's true, why do we so often stick the knife into our own backs?

Sports officials get it from all sides. That's not news. Coaches are on us all game, players beg for calls. And don't even get started on the spectators. We're in enforcement, and like cops and school principals, we're not always super popular.

But nobody does more disservice to officials than officials themselves. From badmouthing each other out of earshot, to cramming our successes down our colleagues' throats, to getting lazy and complacent with our work, to thinking that, "Yeah, I know what's best for this game and I don't care what my bosses or the rules say," as a group we're guilty of sabotage. We torpedo ourselves and then we wonder why we don't get respect.

It's time to take a look at how our attitudes shape our profession and ultimately the games we officiate.

"It's a problem when an official puts him- or herself first and the game second," says Jack Folliard, the executive director of the Oregon Athletic Officials Association, a statewide high school officiating group affiliated with the Oregon School Activities Association. "Our emphasis needs to be on fairly officiating games and not the politics of self-achievement. The guys who hurt officiating are the guys who are more concerned about their career than they are about being the best officials they can be."

It's human nature, of course, and like most other people, we officials tend to focus on ourselves, wonder how we can get an advantage and search for ways to get ahead. A little bit of that is nothing more than being human and, kept in check, it probably doesn't present any serious problems. Left unchecked and allowed to run amok and we have a population of officials whose focus is away from their games and on themselves and inevitably, the games and our avocation suffer.

It's time to take a hard look at where we are and where we're going if we want the best for ourselves. Let's break down the most likely ways in which we, as a profession, can become self-defeating:

GETTING A LITTLE TOO FRIENDLY

An official arrives at a game and immediately makes a beeline for the head coach of the home team. "Hey Bob! How're you doing, pal? How's the team this year? How's your family." Meanwhile that official's partner or partners stand uncomfortably to the side while the conversation deepens. Anybody at the venue, including the opposing team, can see the coach and the official whooping it up like a couple of old college roommates reunited.

Whether it's the officials who get too chatty before the game, the rec league umpires who have beers with the players and coaches after the games or the referees who hang out with players and coaches in the offseason, you can easily lose track and be in danger of giving the perception of favoritism.

"Hey, it's human nature to want to be liked and it's a good thing to develop some rapport with coaches," says Tom Robinson, Colorado High School Athletic Association assistant commissioner in charge of officials. "But it's crucial to make sure everything is fair and looks fair. Whatever talking and kidding you do with one coach you better do in equal amounts with the coach on the other side. Make no mistake, coaches notice everything."

When officials develop an attitude that says, "Hey, I've been doing this so long everyone knows me," you know they're in danger. Familiarity doesn't only breed contempt; it breeds familiarity, and officials who have worked games involving the same participants for a long time can let their guard down. It's as if they've begun to think the rules don't apply to them or they're needy enough that they're looking for friends all over the game.

"Follow what your own organization guidelines and rules say about such things, if there are any, because sometimes it gets very difficult to define. It's tough to say where the line is and when you're crossing it," said Robinson.

It is important to be cordial and it's important to develop relationships but if you want a friend, as Harry Truman said, get a dog.

GOSSIP, SNIPING AND BACKSTABBING

A couple of officials are talking at an association meeting. "Did you hear about Chuck?" says one. "He's going to state."

"You've got to be kidding me," complains the other.

"That guy is worthless."

"You're telling me? You should have seen him work the South game last week. Absolutely pathetic."

Meanwhile, Chuck ambles up to join the conversation. "Hi fellas. What's new?"

"We heard about your state assignment," comes the reply.

"Congratulations, pal. You deserve it, buddy!"

You'll see infighting in lots of different ways. Officials will get the cold shoulder for no good reason. It might mean nitpicking on small things or it could mean petty arguments over something insignificant.

"Sometimes you'll see guys putting down other officials behind their backs to try to elevate their own status," says Folliard. "It's one thing to break down a game — that's a good thing to do — but it's never a good thing to focus on personalities and talk about people who aren't there."

You can want the same successes a fellow official enjoys, but it's something else entirely and much more malevolent to want it and resent your colleague for having it. Sure, you can be disappointed but when you turn that disappointment into hostility toward others you've crossed the line.

LETTING YOURSELF GO

Your crew chief arrives at the game site 20 minutes later than he's supposed to, rushes through a pregame (if he even has one at all), puts on his too-tight uniform, which was new when George H.W. Bush was president and hits the field or court none-too-ready to work the game.

It is our job to treat our work with the appropriate respect. Think back to when you began as an official and remember how you used to do things. You got plenty of rest the night before, you got there early, you looked good and you riveted your attention to the action. You even kept yourself in shape knowing that would impact your performance. That's respect for the game.

How's it different today? Are you pulling in just before the contests start, wiped out from a poor night's sleep, wearing a dirty uniform that doesn't fit anymore because of all the weight you've put on? Professionalism isn't just for the overenthusiastic new guys, it's for everyone, especially for officials who've been doing the work the longest. It's the experienced officials who should know the right way of doing things and who need to lead by example.

SINGING YOUR OWN PRAISES

Local referee makes good and gets tabbed to work games in a big-time college conference. Everyone's happy for the colleague (or not; see the section on "Gossip, Sniping and Backstabbing"). What's the problem? Say the referee still works high school ball in another sport and starts showing up to game sites and association meetings with the college conference logo prominently displayed on her shirt, bag, jacket, even the pen in her pocket. It's not overt, sure, but just to make sure you catch the message, she opens conversation by mentioning how tough things were in her last college game and how that nationally known coach everyone loves is really a big jackass, and oh by the way, she might not be able to make the next association meeting because she's scheduled to work as a clinician at a camp for college hopefuls.

When an official shows up at an assignment armed with the warmup suit, the briefcase and the collection of ballpoints from the last big-time contest he or she's done, what are they really saying? They're saying, "Look how cool I am and how cool you aren't." Sure, there's some room for pride and there's room for passing on experience, but you don't have to have the difference spelled out for you. You know when you're being big-timed and when you're the one without a ton of big-time experience, it's a lonely feeling.

Usually though, big-timing is a much more subtle thing. Sometimes you see it when a team of officials gives the new guy or gal the cold shoulder or doesn't include him or her in pregame conversations. Often it takes place when the big-timing official makes sure he drops all the big games he's done when he's talking to a less-experienced official. When you hear someone say, "You know, I remember feeling a little nervous before my first four state assignments but not anymore." Or, "Boy, the thing I hate about working the conference championship is the travel."

Tony Mariconda is an off-ice NHL official who is also very involved with U.S. Hockey at the amateur level. He also works prep football and softball in New Jersey. His positions in both the pros and the amateurs put him in an interesting position. "I avoid talking about my involvement in the NHL when I'm working an amateur game or doing an officials' seminar," he says. "It has nothing to do with U.S. Hockey and if I went around talking about the NHL all the time, it would easily turn a lot of people off. I feel uncomfortable with it when I'm working as an amateur."

Mariconda plays it smart. The fact is that the other people he works with probably know his NHL experience and they undoubtedly respect it. He lets it speak for itself and in that way he engenders respect for it, not resentment. So much of officiating is about building relationships, and putting yourself above others is not a way to do it.

Playing with the Rules

You're working with an official who claims to be a "Let 'em play type" of referee. Next thing you know, the official is passing on calling fouls left and right, offering up a few warnings here and there even on very obvious infractions that require no judgment. "Aaah! That's a stupid rule anyway," the official explains. Officials have a certain amount of leeway in their interpretation of how the game's rules are to be enforced. A good official has the ability to know when to come down hard with enforcement and when to lay off a bit. However, the official who gets lost in that gray area or begins to define all the rules as gray is doing the game a grave disservice.

"Sometimes (officials) will kind of blend two rules together and take part of one regulation and part of another," says Mariconda. "I've seen it when it comes to enforcing major penalties and game misconducts. It could be something as simple as (officials) not wanting to fill out reports and not wanting to call attention to themselves or their games."

We use our judgment and the flexibility of some rules in ways that benefit the game. If you're bending the rules to make your job easier, to avoid confrontation or to get back at a coach for personal reasons, then you're way out of bounds. It is important to choose your spots and keep the focus on the game because when you play with the rules, the effect can snowball out of control. If you bend something here, pretty soon you may have to bend it back over there, and before you know it your game is all bent out of shape. The results can be embarrassing.

Case in point: "We had a case in girls' softball that got a little crazy," recalls Robinson. "There's a rule about hair barrettes for the players. Well, the umpire noticed one in the last inning of a game in a girl's ponytail and because of it, he disallowed her run and called her out. It made the difference in the game and really approached the absurd."

SUCKING UP

You're milling around chatting with some fellow officials before the start of an association meeting or a rule interpretation meeting when in walks the local assigner. It doesn't take more than a few seconds before you're left chatting with the wall because everyone's glad-handing the assigner.

Can networking be a bad thing? When it's used to enhance knowledge and experience, it betters the game and everyone involved. When it helps you form friendships and partnerships, it's terrific. But when it's used only as a vehicle for personal advancement, it's nothing but shameless self-promotion and politicking.

You can tell the difference without much trouble. When you see

What Do You Do to Sabotage Your Own Career?

A lot of officials are guilty to various degrees of making the larger mistakes of backbiting, politicking, playing fast and loose with the rules. Those are the types of things that make our whole avocation look bad. Here are a few that'll make any individual official look bad:

The poorly thought-out letter
Most states have a formal procedure to send in your comments about an unsportsmanlike act committed by a player or coach. While your responsibility in that area is not to be taken lightly, use it judiciously. Don't write up a player simply because he failed to throw you the ball after a violation was called. Be sure that when you send a letter there is sufficient justification. Let's face it, the more letters the state receives either from or about you, the more it will think that you are the problem, not a player or coach.

A little knowledge can be dangerous
Some officials are too quick to try to prove their legitimacy by enforcing "strange rules." Maybe it's some obscure bit they recently read in the rulebook or heard about at an association meeting. Their immaturity and lack of confidence make those officials look for any opportunity to make a ruling in an attempt to show their expertise and to exercise their power, making something out of nothing and wrecking an otherwise sound game.

Living in denial
It's an embarrassing situation, but what is your first impulse after you realize you've made an obvious mistake during a game? Do you accept responsibility and move on or do you justify it in your own mind or quickly deny that it even happened? In football, for example, it's amazing how many inadvertent whistles "must have come from the stands somewhere." When it's clear to everyone on the field or court that you blew it, you do yourself the most harm by not owning up.

someone who's friendly and conversational with everyone, you can probably make the assumption that official is a gregarious person. If that official is the type who likes to socialize with others and organize everyone to go to dinner or a drink after the game, that's fine too. But when that individual only hangs out with those who can advance his or her career and only makes conversation with the powers that be, it's pretty clear that individual is trying to see just what he or she can get out of the situation.

Why should you care? Because it's another way the integrity of officiating gets threatened. The politickers are doing their best to move up in the ranks not by knowing the game, working hard or demonstrating commitment. They're doing it by kissing up and taking shortcuts. Thankfully, most people can spot disingenuousness fairly quickly so that technique doesn't always work, but occasionally, a very gifted individual with enough schmoozing skills can make his or her way to the top just by making friends. It's discouraging to those who just work hard and show up to do a good job.

"Let's face it, there's ass-kissing on every level," says Robinson. "There's always a battle and if there's a good ol' boy network, that's when you get the worst officiating teams. We address the situation by rotating assignments and we still get guys barking about it. Some guys are never satisfied and can get really irrational about it."

This Isn't It

It's not uncommon for veteran officials to gradually drift away from certain aspects of professionalism. After all, as long as their onfield or oncourt work is exceptional, what's the problem? Plenty. When you start to think you know it all, that you'll always get games because you've been around for so long and the coaches all know you, you're headed for trouble. Those are the same types of officials who haven't read the rulebook in a decade, who don't attend association meetings and who coast along on their past success or reputation.

This Isn't It

Officials who spend too much time rewriting their own rulebooks have lost their way and they put the integrity of the sport in danger. It's faulty interpretations that hurt every official because they make us look unprepared, incompetent and unprofessional. It sabotages everyone who has to make a difficult call, and when the time comes to massage a rule a little bit for the sake of the game, it's going to make it that much harder for the poor official who has to do it right after the official who does it way too much.

This Is It

How do we get ahead as an official while still supporting the sports we serve? Good officials are made from people with good habits, and good habits come from people who try to do good things. Take an inventory of your own behavior and your intentions and you'll have an answer to what we need. Just like every other human endeavor, officiating works best when the people involved are honest, fair and concerned about the welfare of others.

CHAPTER 12

STRONG WORDS

The following advice comes from a number of officials who work varied sports and at different levels. But despite those differences, they share one common quality: wisdom any official can appreciate.

KERMIT QUISENBERRY, FIFA AND MLS ASSISTANT REFEREE

On advancement: "Watch referees whom you respect. If possible, question them as to why they do or don't do certain things. Work hard and work as many games as possible. There are many situations that happen at different levels and by doing that you learn how to handle all of them with all different management skills."

MARGARET DOMKA, FIFA REFEREE

On crew responsibilities: "While each crew member's responsibilities are equally important, a crew can only be successful if they are able to communicate necessary information to each other in appropriate ways and at appropriate times. Essentially, it is the referee's job to make sure that each member of the crew is on the same page regarding what each other's responsibilities are and what the expectations will be for the specific game that is being officiated."

PAT DRISCOLL, NCAA DIVISION I MEN'S BASKETBALL OFFICIAL

On coach interaction: "You've got to show your humanness, be willing to lend an ear and treat them as a professional. I try to keep our conversations succinct and in a professional dialogue."

J.D. COLLINS, NCAA DIVISION I MEN'S BASKETBALL OFFICIAL

On learning from your peers: "Obviously there is a reason some of the major veterans continue to show up in very high-profile games.

They have experienced the atmosphere and know how to handle it. I think as time goes on, I am earning and/or learning some of those things and will continue to learn. I've always told people when I stop learning, then it's time to get out."

JACK FOLLIARD, PAC-12 FOOTBALL OFFICIAL

On earning trust: "I think you have to earn that trust through your own good work on the field, so I try to be the best I can be. I strive to be as knowledgeable about the rules as I possibly can be, and to use the best judgment I can. That's part of leadership. The other way I think you build trust is by always being positive with your crewmates. You can never be negative. Listen to them, let them say what they're thinking and empower them to be able to come up with their own ideas and thoughts."

MIKE WINTERS, MLB UMPIRE

On rekindling your fire: "Sometimes I try and imagine when I umpired as a kid and couldn't wait to get out on the field. Thinking about how much fun it was to umpire, when it wasn't a job, helps to remind me that I am truly fortunate to do what I do for a living,"

ESSE BAHARMAST, FORMER FIFA REFEREE

On giving back to the game: "Service the game at any level. Help out the other referees and have the interest of the game above all else."

ED. T. RUSH, FORMER NBA REFEREE AND DIRECTOR OF OFFICIALS

On people management: "When you first start in the league, you're trying to figure out who the players are and how to make sure you get in the right position. You've only got two responses to conflict. You've got no response or you have a technical foul. As you continue to grow and learn the game and learn the personalities, you develop what I call parents skills. I've got four kids, and I've got probably seven or eight different responses that I have to different behavioral things. It's the same thing on the court. I think we could probably sit down and identify maybe as many as 10 responses to certain situations. If you watch our people, there's a lot of conversation that goes on out there. But it's not flamboyant. They're not throwing their arms up in the air. They're not putting their fingers in people's faces."

TOM LOPES, IAABO EXECUTIVE DIRECTOR AND RETIRED NCAA DIVISION I MEN'S BASKETBALL REFEREE

On being realistic about climbing the officiating ladder: "You have to crawl before you walk. It may not happen tomorrow; it may not happen in five years. I always had hope. No one was ever putting me down as not being able to do those things. After four or five years (of attending a) camp these days, if you don't find yourself getting further along, you might take a look in the mirror and think maybe it's not in the cards."

TONY CORRENTE, NFL REFEREE

On being the face of your league or conference: "At some point every Sunday afternoon, I am the representative of the NFL for three hours. The league turns over the responsibilities of a football game that's worth, to be honest, many billions of dollars … and they say, 'OK, for the next three hours we would sure love it if you would be able to conduct this game in a smooth, rhythmic manner and allow it to be presented in a very positive way."

DONNEE GRAY, NCAA DIVISION I MEN'S BASKETBALL OFFICIAL

On acknowledging the next generation of officials: "Throughout your career, there's always going to be somebody on your tail, coming behind you. I have one of two choices: I can pout or I can pat them on the back and help them and make myself better by being at the camps, learning stuff from them. The reason we say it's competitive is because people are continually coming in. There are people already there and people get better every day."

SONIA DENONCOURT, FIFA INSTRUCTOR AND RETIRED REFEREE

On being consistent: "There's only one way to referee the game: The right way. The rules are clear. If it is a bad tackle, it's a bad tackle. So whoever is playing and however they play, there is one rule and I apply it with what FIFA wants."

BILL LEMONNIER, REFEREE FOR THE 2011 BCS NATIONAL CHAMPIONSHIP FOOTBALL GAME

On using connections to advance your career: "... You do have to have people who will speak on your behalf. What you have to impress those people with is your commitment. You obviously have to show them some ability. Just remember that there's a fine line between the guys who go overboard with calling people and trying to do favors for people to try and move along the way and the guys who are sincerely trying to extract as much good information from experienced people as possible."

JIM BURR, REFEREE FOR SEVEN NCAA DIVISION I MEN'S BASKETBALL FINAL FOURS

On listening to complaints from coaches: "You've got to make it clear to both the coaches what your line in the sand is. I don't believe a coach should be working an official every single time down the court. But I think there are some legitimate times during the course of a basketball game when a coach should bring something that's concerning him to the attention of the official. And if he does that in a professional manner, there's nothing wrong with responding in a professional manner. You may not agree with it, but at least you're listening to his opinion, and I think having that type of relationship between coaches and officials is going to make the game a much better officiated one."

ELIAS BAZAKOS, MLS REFEREE

On working with and trusting crewmates: "Remember that you have assistants, remember that you are part of a team. Even today, if I am at the edge of my comfort zone in a tough game, I remember that we referee as a team, and we all succeed together."